Colin Gibson's

Nature
Diary

Foreword

Flowers, birds and mammals, from mountains, moors and glens, Colin Gibson's weekly Nature Diary emphasised all of these. I always looked forward to reading his articles with their exquisite drawings which rounded off the excellent short story.

I had The Courier delivered to my home in deepest England just to read and admire his work. To have known Colin was one of life's greatest pleasures. He was a quiet and gentle man and to hear him recite the Gaelic poems was always special – they just rolled off his tongue. Colin's vast knowledge of the Scottish countryside is a wonderful legacy left for future generations to browse and read.

Badger Walker
Derbyshire
England

Contents

Foreword – Ray "Badger" Walker

Introduction – Gillian Zealand (nee Gibson)

Introduction

by GILLIAN ZEALAND (nee GIBSON)

Since my father Colin Gibson's death in 1998 I have been asked regularly, "When are you going to publish a collection of his Nature Diaries?"

It was a question my father was often asked too, in his lifetime, by many fans of his weekly column in The Courier.

Well, here it is. No doubt many readers will have their own favourites, and this collection contains a fair number of mine – though, with over 2000 to choose from, many equally appealing ones had to be rejected! I hope the final selection succeeds in capturing something of the spirit of Nature Diary and the range of its subject matter and geography. By adopting a month-by-month format I have tried to suggest the progress of the seasons and to give due regard to notable events in the country calendar; at the same time I have tried to do justice to the huge variety of wildlife and landscape that is ours to savour in 'Courier Country'. Some characteristic anecdotes, observations and reflections, and, of course, the charming black and white drawings, complete, I hope, the Nature Diary 'formula' which has ensured its popularity for over forty years.

This is not, in fact, the first such publication. In the early 1960's the late J. D. Boyd of Dundee Art Galleries and Museums encouraged Dundee Corporation to produce an attractive set of booklets, "Spring", "Summer", "Autumn" and "Winter on Tayside", which reproduced some of my father's early Nature Diary writings. But these have long been out of print, and have become something in the way of collectors' pieces. The present volume should therefore help to fill that gap as well as bringing the collection more up to date.

Colin Gibson was born in Arbroath in 1907 and remained proud of his "Reid Lichtie" roots. During his time at Arbroath High School, he was art medallist and cut his journalistic teeth writing nature notes for the Arbroath Guide. At Gray's School of Art in Aberdeen he won a number of prizes, including two travelling scholarships which took him to Italy and Spain. On his return he was appointed Assistant Art Master at Dundee High School, a post he held for twelve years. But he continued to paint and write; his first book, "The New Furrow", an evocative celebration in words and pictures of the Angus countryside, was published in 1938. After the war he gave up teaching to concentrate on writing and illustrating full time, becoming a regular contributor to such publications as Gamekeeper and Countryside, Trout and Salmon, the Book of the Braemar Gathering and the Scots Magazine, scripting radio programmes and researching a biography of Allan Cameron, stalker on the Balmoral estate.

In 1954 Colin was approached by Iain Stewart, then assistant editor of The Courier, who wanted to introduce a new Saturday feature and suggested half a dozen nature notes "to see how they would go." The first "Colin Gibson's Nature Diary" (without a drawing, incidentally – this was added several issues later) appeared on 2nd October, 1954, its subject the roaring of the stags. So well received was this short run that it was continued and soon became an indispensable part of the Saturday edition.

From the start, Nature Diary displayed that characteristic mix of natural history, topography, country lore, local history and personal anecdotes which has ensured its enduring appeal through several generations of Courier readers. Although, in the course of forty years, Colin inevitably went back over familiar ground, his writing always remained fresh and immediate, his word pictures vivid to the mind's eye and his illustrations beautifully crafted, capturing perfectly the character of a place or the poise of a bird or animal. As well as a wide range of interests he had a remarkably retentive memory and could recall not only people, places, conversations and events but also such things as field names and fishing pools, poetry (lighthearted and serious), sayings and snatches of broad Scots humour. All went into Nature Diary.

His weekly column made Colin many friends, brought numerous visitors to his home in Monifieth and generated a great deal of fan mail, which in turn provided further fuel for his pen. Over the years he met, or corresponded with, like minded people from all over Scotland and well beyond. These included writers such as Capt. W. E. Johns of 'Biggles' fame, Derek Cooper, the well known gourmet, poet Brenda Macrow (with whom he shared a love of the Torridon Highlands), and a whole host of farmers, gamekeepers, stalkers, fishermen, birdwatchers, botanists, hillwalkers and many others who made their living or spent their leisure hours in the Scottish countryside. Another good friend and countryman of many interests, Ray "Badger" Walker from Derbyshire, has kindly written the foreword to this book.

A word about the drawings. Colin's favourite medium for illustrative purposes was "scraperboard" – card covered with a thin layer of plaster of Paris which can be left white or coated matt black. On white scraperboard, drawing is done freehand in ink with a pen or fine brush, and an etching tool is used to cut into the more solid areas of ink to lighten them. On a black ground the drawing is executed with the etching tool itself, cutting through to expose the white plaster beneath; the effect is more formal, something like a woodcut. Either way, the bold black and white drawings which result are ideal for reproducing on newsprint. The following pages contain examples of both black and white scraperboard, although Colin generally preferred to work on white. I have tried for the most part, in making this selection, to choose articles whose original drawings are still extant, although some of these have been modified, or even redrawn, over the years. They are reproduced here closer to actual size than in their reduced Nature Diary format.

This book would not have come about without the encouragement of Ian Lamb of The Courier, who has also offered much practical help and advice. I would also like to express my grateful thanks to D. C. Thomson and Co. Ltd., not only for their co-operation over the reproduction of the texts for this volume but also for their continuing commitment to publishing vintage Nature Diaries in the familiar Saturday slot, to the gratification of my father's many friends and fans.

January

Come into the neuk;
Come awa, come awa,
It blaws baith snell and sair o!
Noo the onding's smoorin hicht and howe,
And the peesie wheeps nae mair o!

DEEP snow everywhere, and wintry skies foretelling more to come! With its sombre trees and its white drifts, Powrie Castle looked the very picture of a medieval dwelling in the long, long ago.

The strong northwest wind had blown much of the dry snow from the upper fields into the roads and hedges, and there were many knife-edged ridges to negotiate.

In the lea of a coppice, eddying gusts had built up fantastic grottoes and minarets of snow, and the firwoods were carrying their heaviest eaves of the winter.

In an interlude of January sunlight it was all very beautiful – the sky a frail blue, tinting to green, the white fields bathed in the light, azure in their hollows.

But the snow picture had its darker side. The trampled and scattered snow by a wood edge showed how desperately a flock of fieldfares or redwings had searched for food there.

Flocks of wood pigeons, too, went straggling over the land, settling hopefully wherever a touch of green betrayed a root crop.

I remember farmer David Pate of Kincreich telling me these "cushie-doos" would go for anything in this hungry weather, even around the steadings; but I noticed them in the hedgerows, too, searching painstakingly for the last of the wild berries, and under trees, searching for beechmast.

Between Powrie Castle (once the home of the Fothringhams) and Craigowl (highest top of the Sidlaws) the slopes looked wintry indeed, with Glen Ogilvy shut away in a fastness of its own.

Oldtime travellers used to go that way between Kirriemuir and Dundee – either on foot or horseback – and in this kind of weather it was a truly perilous undertaking for man and beast.

Apart from the hardy red grouse, and perhaps a hungry fox on the prowl, little would be seen in the way of wildlife at present.

Happily some forms of wildlife suffer less than others. Crossbills find their food among cone-bearing trees, and are not greatly affected by frost and snow.

I came, too, on a sprightly party of bullfinches making a wintry foray through a sheltered belt of trees. The rose-vermilion breasts of the male birds made a vivid colour note where the snow lay in sunlight and the green bark shone.

Jackdaws, starlings, house sparrows, chaffinches – these birds generally find some sustenance around villages and farms; but of a dozen species, including wild geese, fieldfares and redwings, seen at this time of year, probably only the farmyard sparrows are truly resident.

If they survive these hungry months, the others will return in spring to their homelands on the fringes of the Arctic Circle.

Powrie Castle in snow

WHITE hare, blue hare, variable hare, mountain hare, Scottish maukin – call it what you will. If you cross the Hill of Menmuir or the Caterthuns, north-west of Brechin, you are fairly sure to see several of these fleet-footed Highlanders darting away over the snowy slopes.

The scientific name of this hare is Lepus timidus – Latin for hare and timidus for timid.

Yet in my experience this hare is less shy than the common brown hare of the lowland fields and will often betray its presence needlessly through sheer curiosity.

In April (their mating season) they hardly bother to move out of one's way.

Both the Lowland and Highland hares live their lives in the open and depend on their speed of movement to keep them out of danger.

But this hare of the Scottish hills – a smaller, more compact animal – is quite ready to take cover if necessary and has no fault to find with the nearest rock or peat-hag when a golden eagle swings over the skyline.

And this is quite a possible happening in the unfrequented country north of Menmuir and those deep glens of the Westwater and the Paphrie Burn.

The name Paphrie means "the shining one," but with hill and glen wrapped in a snowy mantle the burn shows up as a black furrow, erratically ploughed, down the length of its level glen.

At the glenhead, where it narrows, lie the crags associated with Ledenhendry, the young farmer who led the men of Fern at the affray known as the Battle of the Saughs.

Later in his life Ledenhendry had other enemies and one evening when they lay in ambush he gave them the slip by hiding in a cleft of these rocks, now called Ledenhendry's Chair.

When I was up this way last summer and met shepherd Smith with his fine flock of ewes and lambs the hill slopes were bathed in sunlight and the cuckoo was calling from the brae.

But January brings its own austere landscape – a silent white world with distant trees and crags engraved on the dark sky.

It also brings down the starving deer-herds and along this fringe of the Highlands a farmer may well find acres of his turnip crop devastated in a night.

Below Ledenhendry's crag, where the rushing burn loses its voice suddenly in the levels of the glen, there are traces of an old croft – one of many former habitations in the few miles westwards of Lethnot.

A delightful place in June, with its nearby waterfalls and its little wood of aspen trees.

But how isolated these crofters must have felt when snow, whipped by the winter wind, drifted deep around sheep-bucht and byre and the sombre sky over the Caterthuns foretold more snow to come!

Mountain hare

WINTRY weather or no, those hardy annuals, the rod and line fishers of the Tay, got off to a fair start on January 15.

You need enthusiasm and a hardy constitution for this sport.

But now's the time, if you want to grass a Tay salmon at its best – like a bar of silver, deep-keeled, lusty and fresh from the sea.

After all, the season of the "springers" doesn't last so very long.

"Ye may put yer rod awa' when the May flourish is oot."

Or so they told me along by Stanley, and they should know.

Angling for an early spring fish means spinning nowadays, and often that entails "trolling" from the stern of a boat waiting for a fish to strike, while the ghillies dexterously manoeuvre the boat near favourite "lies."

Success is largely dependent on the oarsmen's knowledge of the pools and currents.

The Tay is the most powerful river in this country.

It has the voice of a great river, that changes little though it reflects a thousand skies.

It has the grace and dignity of a big river.

John Ruskin spent part of his early life on Tayside, and he wrote: "I spent my days here with perpetual watching of all the ways of running water, a regular awe developing in me of the pools of Tay, where water changed from brown to blue black."

Though pre-eminently a writer, Ruskin's studies of rocks and pools are wonderfully impressive in tone and line. "Pools of pausing," he called the river's quieter reaches.

Many of the Tay fishing beats are world-famous.

There are Stanley and Benchill, with the great "Pitlochrie Pool" and the red rocks of Horsey.

There's Catholes and Stobhall, Islamouth and Kenmore, where the salmon sometimes "queue up" in the shadows of the trees, before moving upriver to enter Loch Tay.

As with all salmon rivers, many of the pools have traditional names, like Thistlebrig, Ship Linn, Neil's Head, Sprinty and Tail of Horsey.

In character they vary greatly.

At Stormontfield and Logierait the Tay is on its best behaviour, sedate and orderly, with here and there a peaceful backwater.

At Aberfeldy it runs swiftly and with purpose, and at Campsie Linn it breaks into turbulence.

But smooth or rough, gliding or raging down, it remains a fascinating river.

And it is not to be wondered at that anglers return to it season after season, whatever the early year brings in the way of weather.

A Ghillie on the Tay

GALES involving forest destruction have punctuated the history of our woodlands.

In our own time the year 1968 brought a very destructive storm, when whole swathes of woodland trees were laid low by the scythe of the wind.

But that January day 15 years earlier – and exactly 28 years ago today – is still remembered by forestry men as "the day the forests fell."

It happened on January 31, 1953, and the havoc was caused in a few short hours during daylight.

The north wind came down like a wolf on the fold, and was at its most ferocious at noon, raging through Tayside and the whole north-east of Scotland.

In Perth it "yowled up frae the vennel'd toun"; in Dundee it roared over Balgay and the Law, and hurled debris from the rooftops into the city streets.

In the countryside, even alongside woods, the sound of falling trees was drowned by the howling of this giant wind.

From the first it was realised by foresters that heavy damage was certain, but telephone inquiries and reconnaissance by car were frustrated by fallen wires and tree-blocked roads.

However, it didn't take long to discover that forest damage was on a disaster scale.

Whole woods were flattened, and many country folk can still recall the scenes at such places as Caddam (Kirriemuir), Lintrathen, Carrot Hill and Bachnagairn, at the head of Glen Clova.

A gale of this dimension was bound to glut the timber market, and timber merchants in the area could not possibly handle the amount of fallen timber in an acceptable time.

It was reckoned that 50,000,000 cubic feet of timber had been laid low!

However, firms from farther south gave a helping hand, and everyone in the timber trade responded well.

Outlying forests, difficult of access, were dealt with last, and Bachnagairn was one of these.

The larchwoods there lay far up the course of the South Esk, and to reach them was but the roughest of footpaths, under the rock-scarps of Juan Jorge and the Back Corries.

These woods had for many years been regarded as something of a forestry miracle, for they extended over rugged hill-ground at a height of 1700 feet – much higher than seemed possible for larches to grow and thrive.

When I visited Bachnagairn in the aftermath of that great storm, I found it almost impossible to find a way through the tangle of fallen trees, and it was quite an adventure, trying to find the bridge above the waterfall that carries the track towards Sandy Hillock and Loch Muick.

It was several years later that foresters finally bulldozed a broader track up the riverside.

And although this did nothing to improve the scenery, it did at least allow access to the ravished woods.

"The Day the Forests Fell"

February

Over the land freckled with snow half-thawed
The speculating rooks at their nests cawed

And saw from elm-tops, delicate as flower of grass,
What we below could not see, Winter pass.

THESE lines by Edward Thomas came to my mind when I heard rooks cawing from their rookery trees at Barry. With a northerly wind bringing flurries of February snow, it was too early and too wintry for them to be nest-building.

No doubt they had merely looked in to see how last year's nests had fared in recent storms. Strong as rooks' nests are, probably few had survived.

Yet February, for all its vagaries of weather, is a forward-looking month, and in its more genial interludes it clearly foretells the ever-returning enchantment of spring.

Already I had noticed aconites, snowdrops and crocuses in flower. And now, best of all, I heard a mistle-thrush piping out his far-carrying notes from a tall tree over by the Old Manse.

A true "stormcock," he proclaimed his message in defiance of that piercing wind and drift of snow.

The Old Manse of Barry was, incidentally, the birthplace of John Kirk, who grew to be something of a stormcock himself.

He had an interesting career. At Edinburgh University he was a fellow-student in medicine of the future Lord Lister.

In the Crimean war he defied danger as a medical officer, and later defied dangers of a different kind as chief officer, naturalist, botanist and medical officer on David Livingstone's famous 1853-1864 expedition into the heart of the dark continent of Africa. Later again, as consul-general of Zanzibar, his determination brought an end to the slave trade.

Barry Mill and Den hardly looked their best on this wintry day, though it was sheltered there, with the shut-off wind venting its spite harmlessly in the treetops.

And it pleased me to think that in a few short weeks these banks and braes would be studded with primroses, with here and there a fresh green clump of that curious plant called cuckoo-pint, a rather rare wild flower of this area.

When I returned to the village the snow showers had passed, the sky had cleared, and the wind had fallen. Far to the south, a great bank of cloud had caught the brief bloom of a February sunset.

And there was that thrush again – that herald of spring – back on his lofty perch, pealing out his wild lay.

I stood listening for a little in that magical extension of daylight now recaptured from the winter darkness.

The poet Keats once wearily left his studies to listen to a thrush, and interpreted its song as an admonishment –

O fret not after knowledge – I have none,
And yet my song comes native with the warmth.
O fret not after knowledge – I have none,
And yet the Evening listens…

Mistle-thrush ("Stormcock")

February fill the dyke
Be it black or be it white

UNFORTUNATE **February! How often the second month is left with a legacy of January snow and rain that her rivers cannot cope with.**

How often, in upper Glen Clova (a glen over-deepened by glacial action) the South Esk invades the level haughs below Braedownie, while in Strathmore, the Isla, notorious as a flooding river since prehistoric times, has a habit of losing itself this month in lakes extending over wide areas of farmland, leaving its normal channel marked only by trees and drowning bushes.

What happens to the riverside wildlife at times like these?

Birds are not endangered, and apparently some animals have built-in weather warning systems.

At Jordanstone, near Alyth, I remember the late Sir James Duncan telling me about the Isla rats.

"An ordinary spate doesn't trouble them," he said, "but they seem to know when the river is going to overflow.

"Twenty-four hours before it does, they all migrate to the higher ground around the farms. How they know the river is going to overflow is uncanny.

"The rabbits that burrow in the river banks have no such fore-knowledge. They stay put and pay the penalty."

Although these lowland lakes and brown, turgid rivers alter the look of a landscape, and have a considerable effect on it, the full violence of these winter spates becomes more obvious in the upper reaches of the river.

On the Isla the great fall of Reekie Linn is impressive at any season.

Normally, as in my sketch, this is a double fall and a very beautiful one. But in full February spate, Reekie Linn is a truly awe-inspiring spectacle.

The two falls form into a fearsome cataract of nearly 100 feet and the thunderous roar of the water crashing into its dark ravine can be heard, as its "reek" may be seen, over a mile away.

Such floods must carry thousands of tons of our soil seawards.

Some of it will no doubt be left on river banks and water meadows, and may improve fertility.

But much of it will be borne to the estuaries, licking out in long, brown tongues into the sea, and mingling with the sand to form new banks and shoals.

So nature creates as it destroys and we, in watching the swirling waters race past, witness our very fleeting portion of the eternal task.

Reekie Linn

THERE is no need to scale mountains to find outstanding viewpoints in our part of the country. Those who "hike or bike," as well as car-tourists, can find them at road level.

The road over Carrot Hill, for instance, is easily reached from Broughty Ferry or Monikie, and at its highest point, where the land falls away sharply towards the north-west, it gives a magnificent widespread view. Part of that view is shown in my drawing.

Again, over in Fife, the road that crosses Walton Hill (a mile or two west of Chance Inn village) presents an unexpected vista of the Lomonds and the Eden Vale, overwhelming in its beauty.

Tullybaccart, on the Dundee-Coupar Angus road, is another good viewpoint, and even Queen Victoria had her carriage halted here, so that she might dwell for a little on the sunlit landscape of Strathmore and the distant Highland hills.

Still another spot that always calls for a halt on my part is on the old Forfar-Brechin road, a mile or two east of Aberlemno and its famous Pictish stones. This view embraces the valley of the South Esk, with the woods and fields of Marcus and Balglassie, and the Braes of Angus rising in a wilder hinterland to the north.

Then a road near The Gask, a fine old-established farmstead set between Cononsyth and Bractullo Bridge ("Brackley Brig") in the Letham district, is a viewpoint with a pleasant surprise.

In clear weather the Perthshire peak of Schiehallion becomes visible in the distant west – blue as a flower in the summer light, and at this time of year still white with winter snow.

But to return to Carrot Hill. My drawing shows but a limited sector of a wide expanse that ranges from the hills of Fife to the nearer heights of the Sidlaws, to the fair lands of Fothringham and Lour, with mansions and farms etched delicately here and there.

But it is the long broken line of the Grampians that holds the eye, with the White Mount of Lochnagar rising "abune them a'."

White Mount is the name now applied to Lochnagar's broad southern slope, but at one time this was the name given to the whole mountain.

From Carrot Hill the famous north-east corrie with its dark crags is hidden, and so is that still darker loch that the young Lord Byron called "Lachin y Gair" in his well-known verses, later set to music with the title "Dark Lochnagar."

What does the name Carrot mean? Obviously, it has nothing to do with vegetables. In an earlier Gaelic form it may well have been Carrait, meaning simply rocky land.

But the "carr" might also have referred to a fortification on the crown of the hill, in those days when its adversaries were more than wild winds and drifting snow.

Wintry view from Carrot Hill

FINDING a viewpoint for portraying a farmhouse at close range is not always easy. And sketching in a pasture where cattle are grazing is (as I have discovered before now) liable to become less a calling than a pursuit!

Scottish farmhouses – sturdily-built of the native stone, or gleaming through their trees with a white roughcast of harling – seem to acquire merit with age.

The older they are, some of these farm-touns (and however out of date by modern standards of efficiency), the better they seem bedded into the Scots lowland landscape.

The viewpoint difficulty can sometimes be solved by getting a bit of height. I painted one farm from the roof of a byre, another from a tree.

And twice (at Bonhard and Hatton of Carsegray) I worked precariously perched on the top of a pair of steps.

Time of year, and of day, has a good deal to do with the look of a farmstead. A white farmhouse may sparkle in spring sunshine, but it will look desolate in snow.

Again, a farm facing east will be left in shadow by the westering sun. Then a farm in a setting of trees will probably look its best in spring or autumn, for the heavy leafage of summer may obscure too much.

Some farms have a more picturesque setting than others. I never take the rough road from Denmark to Leysmill without pausing to admire Newton of Boysack, shown in my sketch with its rushy pond and its tall trees caught in February sunlight.

I mentioned Denmark – a curious name. John Carrie, a 19th century antiquarian, mentions that a military camp stood here, believed to be Danish, but demolished before his time.

Leysmill, too, is deep-rooted in the past. Several tumuli excavated here have yielded "dwarf graves" and sepulchral urns.

Then, in the 15th century, a skirmish between those feuding families of the Scottish nobility, the Lindsays and the Ogilvys, which began at the gate of Arbroath Abbey, was fought to a finish in these marshy fields – "the Battle o' the Leys" they called it in after years.

With its pavement quarries, its lint-mill, its inn and its railway station Leysmill was once a brisk little place. But all these are likewise things of the past.

I had a ramble round the reedy pools and wooded ridges eastwards of the village – once a favourite duck-shooting haunt of that airman and sporting writer, the late Terence Horsley.

After recent floods the willows by the water stood like old crones in fringed shawls, but a wild currant bush had already caught the first clear sunshine of early spring in its mesh of crimson twigs.

At a reedy inlet free of ice I rose several mallard, teal and tufted duck.

Waterhens went tugging away and in the alder thickets were many smaller fry – finches, tits and buntings.

The lengthening of the day, with that extension of twilight so magically recaptured from the winter darkness, was very noticeable.

But the higher ground still lay in snow and the sunset sky of primrose chilling to aquamarine foretold a keener frost to come.

Newton of Boysack, Angus

March

"**B**LAW the weather as it likes, there's bield about Pitmilly's dykes." And just as well there is, for easterly winds like we had last week are hard to thole along by St Andrews' Kinkell Braes and Buddo Ness!

Even those hardiest of sea-going duck, the eiders, seemed to have their shoulders more hunched than usual as they huddled together in that bitter blast – "a wind like a whetted knife," if ever there was one.

On the foreshore I am always tempted to have another look at that curious upstanding geological formation known as the Rock and Spindle.

As shown in my sketch, it lords it over the other ash-grey rocks of the beach, about a mile beyond St Andrews' East Sands.

I think geologists all agree that it is of volcanic origin, as Sir Archibald Geikie claimed late in the 19th century. The cliffs beyond Elie and that notable Fife eminence, Largo Law, seem also to have a volcanic history.

It was hardly a day for the seaside, but at least there was plenty to see and hear in the way of coastal birds.

I noticed quite a large gathering of oystercatchers, heard the treble-notes of redshank farther out and the wilder alarm-call of curlew.

Farther along several cormorants rested and digested their last meal alongside breaking waves.

From the clifftop above the Rock and Spindle a track leads inland towards Kinkell Farm and two miles beyond this lies the ancient village of Boarhills.

Its church, a notable landmark on the higher ground, stands like a sentinel guarding both village and the lower vale of Kenly Burn.

Boarhills, despite its up-to-date look, is deeply rooted in the past and some of its cottages are said to be several centuries old.

At one time the titles of the Bishops of St Andrews included that of Lord of Boarhills, and at Kenly Green, alongside the burn, formerly stood Inchmurtach Palace, a favourite resort of these ecclesiastics.

Here the bishops feasted royalty on many occasions and it was to Inchmurtach that King David the Second (son of Robert the Bruce) brought his child queen, himself a boy of eight years.

I said the view from Boarhills Church was impressive. But the view that lingers in the memory is of St Andrews itself as seen from Kinkell Ness, with, near at hand, the fretted sea breaking into foam and beyond that the tower of St Rule and the cathedral ruins rising boldly into the troubled sky.

The early history of St Andrews is shrouded in its own "haar" of tradition and legend, but we can at least believe that thereabouts lay the cave –

> *Where good St Rule his holy lay,*
> *From midnight to the dawn of day,*
> *Sung to the billows' sound.*

The Rock and Spindle

The pike, the puddock and the perch
A' spaan i' the month o' Merch

SO says an old nature rhyme. The rook, too, begins to look with a speculative eye at what remains of last year's nests in the swaying branches of the rookery wood.

Rooks are firmly established in their ways. They maintain the same close community at all seasons and no doubt this continuity of social life has had its influence on what might be called their tribal customs.

It's fascinating to watch these birds at nesting time. Some of them labour industriously. Others (the males possibly) seem to spend most of their time lustily cawing.

In building they obviously prefer pliant growing sticks to dry dead ones. They will perch precariously on tossing branches, craning forward with open wings and fanned-out tail, determinedly trying to break off twigs they specially wanted.

To prefer pliant twigs to brittle ones is understandable, but the ways of rooks are not always so easy to fathom. They are never sweir to hold a "parliament" or "craw court" to discuss things and, if necessary, to take disciplinary measures against any rook transgressing the rookery laws.

One bird, perching alongside her nest, was suddenly encircled by other rooks and made to dismantle the whole structure. Several times this unfortunate bird tried to fly away, but was herded back. She was kept there until, stick by stick, she had taken the nest to pieces and not a stick remained.

One can only guess at the reason for that sort of behaviour.

Rooks have gone down in numbers greatly in recent years and what were formerly busy rookery woods now stand silent and deserted.

At one time, eastern Scotland had a far greater density of rooks than any other area in Great Britain or outside it. This in spite of the fact that Scotland is the most northerly country wholly included within the rook's breeding range.

I once took upon myself the task of locating all the winter roosts and rookeries in Angus.

Each winter roost had its "parish" of satellite rookeries, populated only from spring to autumn. But even the location of some of the winter roosts was puzzling and led me a dance over the whole of Angus – and beyond!

I discovered, for instance, that the rooks that foraged along the Dighty valley drifted away westwards at dusk and roosted in Perthshire. Carnoustie's rooks went north to a winter roost in the Guynd's Black Den, Carmyllie. But one lot joined a Barry flock and spent their winter nights in trees on Buddon moor.

Another flock from Barry flew west at sunset, crossed the Tay and roosted in Fife. Only when their nests were built did they settle down in Angus!

Rooks building

SOON the catkins of the "pussy willow," cradled on the winds of spring, will be changing from silver to gold.

Almost all our native trees are catkin bearers – oak, alder, birch, hazel, willow, poplar and aspen.

But these "pussy willows" of the saugh or goat willow are the ones that most catch the eye.

It's a curious habit, this, of putting out flowers before leaves.

But in every case the reason seems to be the same.

The trees and plants concerned are mainly wind-fertilised, and this practice allows the wind-borne pollen to float on the air unhindered by foliage.

Even at that, great quantities of this dusty pollen must be produced, for trees of similar kind may be a fair distance away.

And furthermore, the wind is a wasteful carrier.

I mentioned the aspen. It's a tree less commonly seen in these parts than other hardwoods, yet it occurs in a few of our Highland glens.

When I followed the Paphrie Burn from Bridgend of Lethnot to that craggy little glen where it comes bickering down from Peat Hill, I came upon a grove of aspens growing on a sheltered bank above the cascades and brown pools of the burn.

Though there are traces of old crofts hereabouts, I doubt if these aspens were ever planted by man.

Hazels grow up this way, too.

Their catkins, dangling loosely in the hill winds, are often called by children "lammies' tails."

The aspen is, in summer, notable for its fluttering leaves.

They are set on long flexible stalks, and they move and tremble even when the leaves of other trees hang motionless.

These lines by Sir Walter Scott come readily to mind –

> And variable as the shade
> By the light quivering aspen made.

A lesser poet (Lightfoot) tells of –

> One tree the solemn quiet breaks
> Whose quivering foliage cannot rest…

The hazel, too, often enters into verse, and Scott writes memorably of "lone Glenartney's hazel shade."

Lone Glen Paphrie's hazel coppices are much less extensive, but equally delightful.

Catkins

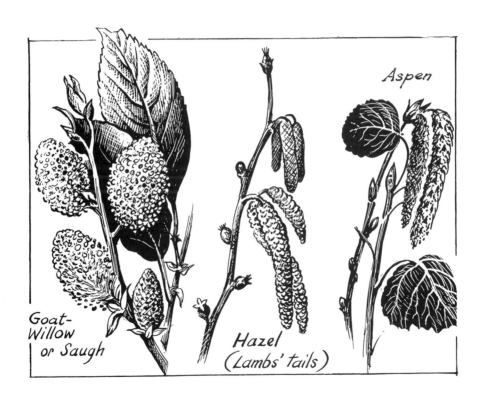

Goat-Willow or Saugh

Hazel (Lambs' tails)

Aspen

There's night and day, brother, both sweet things;
sun, moon and stars, brother, all sweet things;
there's likewise a wind on the heath. Life is very
sweet, brother.

THESE **immortal words of Jasper Petulengro from that strangely fascinating book, Lavengro (by George Borrow) never fail to come to my mind when I cross Rossie Moor, over towards Montrose.**

Follow the rough track that skirts the broad marsh called Nicholl's Loch, and you know all about that wind on the heath. Especially on an early spring day!

Before the word cadger came down in the world to mean a vagrant or scrounger, it meant a carrier or purveyor.

And this moorland track over Rossie Moor was part of the Cadger's Road, the right-of-way by which the Royal Cadger took a supply of fresh fish every morning from the beach at Usan, on the Angus coast, to Forfar – this to supply the royal table, when early Scottish kings and their courts were in residence in the castle there.

In mid-March, moorfowl such as teal and mallard begin to return to these upland moors. So do snipe, and the long-sustained trill of the curlew captures again the spirit of these lonely windswept places.

Though they will not nest until May, blackheaded-gulls are already drawing nearer and nearer to the nesting lochans they claim as their own. Beautiful birds these – white, with a mantle of silver-grey and wings tipped with black.

At this time, they don the black (or, more accurately, chocolate-brown) hood that gives them their name.

When nesting does begin, so does the excitement. Intruders are met with a deafening battle-cry and birds swooping down aggressively. The threat is no more than a threat, but all the same I once got my hat knocked off here!

At one time this district gave a living to several hundred country folk, mainly working with flax, which was soaked, or retted, in the moorland lochans, then processed further in a nearby water-mill.

Another mill, dealing with grain, stood at the head of Den of Fullerton (on the north side of the moor), and there was also a castle, later survived only by a doocot in a field near Bonnington Farm, on the Montrose-Forfar road.

But long, long before then, men of the Stone Age knew these upland moors as a hunting-forest, and it's still possible to find traces of their activities in the shape of spear and arrowheads.

I once had the luck to find one of these flinty arrowheads at an old rabbit warren requisitioned by stock-doves for nesting.

It lay in the loose sand at the mouth of a burrow, showing that rabbits, in their "digs," can be helpful "archaeologists" at times!

The shelter afforded by Pamphrie Wood, on the western fringes of the moor, is lost again on the way downhill to Farnell, with the wind on the heath in cold pursuit.

No doubt these primitive hunters of prehistoric times snuffed that self-same wind. Perhaps they, too, felt that life was sweet as they trudged homeward after a successful foray in quest of moorfowl and the bounding roe.

Blackheaded gulls

April

APRIL – proverbially fickle in its weather – is the lambing month of the Blackface ewes, the little grey sheep of the hills. And it's a queer harvest, the hill-lambing – a trying time for the folk of the hill-crofts as well as for their flocks.

If snowstorms come, as they so often do in the Highlands in early April, and bring with them those icy blasts of the "teuchat storms," it takes determined efforts to save the "yowes," now heavy with lamb.

With the untiring help of the faithful collies, they'll be gathered in to the shelter of the buchts and the drystane dykes. Some may have to be dug out of drifts. Weakly lambs may have to be brought indoors and bottle fed, motherless lambs fostered on another ewe whose own lamb has died.

I can tell you, the hill-shepherd and his wife often get little sleep and hardly a square meal till the crisis is past.

Another danger at this time are the hill-foxes.

Whether these Highland foxes actually kill many lambs is a debatable subject. The remains seen at a den may well be those of still-born lambs found in the pastures.

But all the same, if a shepherd sees a ewe with a young lamb in the gloaming of an April day and then, in the morning, finds a frantic ewe and no lamb, he has no illusions.

The legendary fox of the Scottish Highlands was called the red-legged fox, and it was virtually extinct about the middle of last century. This animal was stronger, and longer in the leg, than the "hill-tod" of present time, and, like the wolf, the red-legged fox was a menace to sheep farmers.

Nevertheless, the hill-foxes of today are certainly bigger animals than the English fox and a Scottish dog-fox may weigh 20 pounds or even more.

Foxes are not often seen in daylight, and when they show themselves they are usually mobbed by birds.

Oystercatchers – noisy birds at any time – will put the whole riverside on the alert if they discover a fox lurking in a bed of rushes near their nesting territory.

Jays will escort a fox through a plantation, swearing at him all the way in their harsh jay language.

Carrion-crows and ravens will dive-bomb any fox that trespasses on a hillside they regard as their own.

Another give-away sign is a musty smell among bushes or bracken where a fox recently hid or passed by.

The fox's survival is as much due to quick thinking as to his turn of speed; but he can travel very swiftly, making light of dykes and fences. If necessary he will swim freely and strongly.

Foxes are good parents and if, by some chance, the vixen is killed, the dog-fox will take over, working himself to a shadow in the rearing of the cubs.

These fox cubs, like the two in my drawing, are as delightful in their own way as the lambs of the Blackface sheep. But little do they know, at this stage, that the hand of man is against them!

Fox cubs

IN a recent report of a hang-gliding experiment at Barry/Buddon it was said that an electric winch was used to launch the glider, "as this area has no hills."

Well, admittedly, it has no height above 100 feet, but it is certainly not as dead flat as aerial photographs suggest.

What of the Barry Ridge, the Hog's Back, the Green Braes, the Pinnacle, North Hill, the Lighthouse Bluff, the Sandy Downs, and those isolated tops, St Helena and Spion Kop?

In the cool of evening, when a ground mist forms on the links and moorland-marshes, these eminences stand above the layer of white like an archipelago of islands in a calm sea.

There are also some delightful valleys (one called Happy Valley), sheltered from the winds and the east coast haar by sturdy Scots pines and thickets of willow and sea-buckthorn.

"We have a sea near us, the Firth of Tay," once wrote Thomas Erskine, of Linlathen, in a letter to his friend, the great Thomas Carlyle, "along which runs for many miles delicious links of sweet sward and most fantastical miniatures of hills and valleys, through which I used to walk and ride…"

During his long reign as lighthouse-keeper, the late Charles Liness often showed me round his vegetable garden, which was sunken and protected from the gales by a feal-dyke, or turf-wall.

A strip of conifers was also planted at one time to give the house and its precincts more shelter, but many of these trees have suffered badly from the winter gales. Now, a stout fence encloses the whole area.

Recently, I had a query about a stone standing at a corner of this fence – obviously a boundary-stone, as it has the letter M inscribed on one side, and SF on the other.

This is quite a historic stone, dating back to the 17th century. M stands for Maule (of Panmure) and SF for Seaman Fraternity.

It was then that George, Third Earl of Panmure – a very public-spirited nobleman – feued to the Seaman Fraternity of Dundee the ground upon which they erected "the lights of Tay," the lighthouses which for many years proved so useful to ships entering this difficult and dangerous firth.

For this, he charged a ground annual of only 5s.

Another stone, similarly inscribed, but more than half buried in the sandy turf, stands near the "low" lighthouse.

Probably others could be found, marking the limits of the ground in question, but stones (and even buildings) have a habit of disappearing out this way, where the land as well as the channels, banks and "swatchways" of the Tay estuary is very much the prey of wind and moving sand.

Incidentally, an eider-duck made her nest alongside the first of these historic stones some years back.

Miss Mary Troup, then housekeeper at Buddon Ness lighthouse, showed it to me, and my sketch shows the duck on her nest of eiderdown.

Eider and historic stone

FOR those who like to travel slowly, and preferably on foot, the little glens of the Carse Braes have much to commend them.

A few days ago, with my daughter for company, I visited Pitroddie and its glen – surely one of the most charming recesses of the Sidlaws.

Plots of daffodils gave us a springtime welcome, and birds were in full song as we took the narrow, steep road that leads to Pitroddie Farm.

If you're up this way, notice (at the right-hand side of the road near some sheds) the model of a medieval castle – all battlemented, red-turreted, moated and drawbridged – skilfully worked in cement on a cairn of stones. Who was the artist-architect?

I do not know, but a German prison camp was established here at one time, and probably one of the prisoners of war bequeathed his memory of a castle on the Rhine to the Braes of the Carse.

After all, the castle fragment on Kinnoull Hill was inspired in much the same way.

Farther up the glen we passed a line of quarrymen's cottages.

Much quarrying was done at one time along this hill-face, and geologically the landscape is of great interest.

Actually the burn follows the line of a major "fault" through the Sidlaws, and a massive dolerite "dyke" towers over it for a long way.

We found this cliff (shown in my sketch) alive with jackdaws and stockdoves, many of them nesting in inaccessible crevices of the rock face above earth-falls and fans of scree.

Beyond these rocks, steep, whinny slopes lead to the summit of Evelick Hill, one of the great viewpoints of the Sidlaw range.

The hill is crowned with ancient earth-works and in its day must have been an impregnable stronghold, defended by steep rocks on two sides and by ramparts and ditches where the crags ease off into grass and heather.

From the turfy rim we had a tremendous view – the whole Carse spread before us, much of "The Kingdom," and inland the snow-flecked Grampians, with Ben Lawers and Schiehallion "abune them a'."

Nearer at hand – in fact, right below us on the east – lay Evelick Castle and farm.

Centuries ago Evelick was the fortified home of the Lindsays, and a fine old song tells of Sir Alexander Lindsay's lovely daughter, "Bonny Leezie Lindsay," on whom a local laird had set his heart.

But the lady prefers another – a wanderer, who later proves to be a clan chief in disguise.

> *Will ye gang to the Highlands, Leezie Lindsay,*
> *Will ye gang to the Highlands wi' me?*
> *For I am Lord Ronald McDonald,*
> *A Chieftain o' high degree.*

From Evelick Hill my daughter (who also has a will of her own) commanded that we should visit nearby Pole Hill before descending.

So, with grouse rising from the heather, we made for this higher summit, which bears a few wind-twisted pines and stunted oaks, and a gleaming white survey triangulation pedestal.

From there a glancing shower drove us down, but the sun was shining and the curlews trilling again long before we reached the Pitroddie Burn and made our way back to the levels of the Carse.

Geological fault, Pitroddie (Carse Braes)

Dear Colin, like mony anither body
I thank ye for yer nature study;
Mony a year back my mind did turn
When ye wrote aboot the Vinney Burn.

THESE were the first lines of an epistle in verse sent me some time ago by a Perth reader. Now, here am I writing about Vinneyside again.

This time I followed the stream down from Craichie, where an inn and a cluster of cottages stand on "the broo o' a stey brae." The burn is "gey sma'" so near its source, but it's a great haunt of waterhens, water wagtails and water voles. I put up a heron on my way down to Bractullo Bridge – Brackley Brig, it usually gets.

There used to be a line of great willows spaced out alongside the water at this part. When they were felled it was like losing old friends. These grand old trees – they gave identity to the place, and how bare and desolate it looked without them!

There is a personality about trees, and seeing them year in year out one almost comes to greet them, especially on a spring morning when the peewits are tumbling over the fallow land and life begins to stir in every wood and field.

They never seemed to grow in size, these willows – I mean as a larch plantation might tower up to 30 or 40 feet in the same number of years – yet they seemed to mature in some way.

In summer, this was an almost sure find for spotted-flycatchers. I used to watch them twisting and turning in pursuit of some insect they had marked down, then returning to some favoured perch by the stream.

Trout, too, were fond of the willows, and many a "souster" lurked in the shadows where branch and leaf dipped in the water. Two of the first trout I ever caught were taken here, with a borrowed "wand," casting under the trees. Speckled beauties, I can still remember them!

But when the trees went, the trout went, too. Plenty of leaf and weed-cover, freedom from pollution – these are the things that count on such streams, rather than restocking.

Farther down, I nearly stepped on a nesting wild duck – the eggs "weel happit" in soft grey down and withered fern. Other early nesters were dippers and stock doves.

Leaving the Den, it was interesting to revisit Letham. Despite a few changes, the square contrives to look much as it did in those almost legendary days when the horse-brake used to ply to and from the railhead at Aldbar.

I thought of the "flooer show" of John Young, the scholarly registrar who spoke several languages but wrote in guid Lowland Scots; and of the old lady who looked at an early motor car rattling across the square and said, "Ye ken, thae things'll kill somebody wan day."

With evening gathering up the sky I made for the dark and haunted Hill of Dunnichen. Beyond it I could see the lights of Forfar twinkling in the April dusk.

A fine pair of trout

May

❧

WITH the orchards of Gowrie coming into blossom, and clouds like pennants flying on the roadsteads of the sun, I took the road from Glencarse to St Madoes and that quaint old-world village called Cottown.

To follow this road is like going back through the centuries. From the roaring traffic of the Perth-Dundee main road it's only a few hundred yards – but also a thousand years! – to the ancient Hawk's Stone of the Hays of Errol.

This boulder that raises a rugged shoulder in a cottage garden has fascinating associations with events of the tenth century.

At that time Danish invaders had left a trail of death and desolation right from their landing-place at Montrose through Angus and the lands of Tayside.

King Kenneth halted them at Luncarty, and at a crucial stage of the conflict a peasant named Hay and his sons left their work in the fields and took up arms – with such fervour that they turned the whole tide of battle in favour of the Scots.

Kenneth acknowledged his debt to these peasant-warriors, and later he granted Hay as much land "on Tay in Gowrie" as a hawk, set free, should fly over before settling. The bird made a wide sweep, and settled on this stone.

Cottown's associations with the past are less legendary and more apparent.

Wandering through the village I found the metalled road dwindling to a dusty track, then losing itself altogether near the reedy shores of the Tay, directly opposite Newburgh.

Cottown's cottages – one is shown in my sketch – are thatched and well worth seeing – trim, well cared for, and set in delightful flower gardens.

Older still are several houses now used mainly as sheds and storehouses. These date back to the 17th century, are reed-thatched and still partly walled in clay.

They stand as mementoes of an architecture peculiar to the Carse of bygone days, and are still in fairly good repair.

Cottown had at one time its blacksmith, joiner, grocer, tailor, schoolma'am and its weavers.

Nearby stood a brick and tile works, and it's recorded that the bricks required in building both the first and second Tay bridges were made here.

Older still is a tradition of these parts that the River Tay at one time flowed much nearer the Braes of the Carse than it does now, and an old ballad persists (in the haunting way that ballads can!) that –

> *The stannin' stanes o' Semmiedores
> Be sou' the River Tay...*

Semmiedores (curiously reminiscent of Lindores, across the Firth) is still the local pronunciation for St Madoes, and evidence from various parts of the Carse suggests that the tradition holds more than an inkling of the truth.

A cottage at Cottown

UP he rose as I came round a bend of the river – all neck and legs and beating wings. Then he pulled himself together, drew in his yellow bill, and flapped leisurely away. In this country we have only one member of the stork family. That's the heron.

It's said that there are about 4000 breeding pairs, spread thinly over most counties between Caithness and Cornwall.

In our part of the country, outwith the nesting season, herons can sometimes be seen in fair numbers at Edenmouth and Lintrathen.

And in Angus there used to be sizeable heronries at Montreathmont, Pitleavie, Letham Grange and Ethie Woods.

In recent years, however, only a few isolated nests, or groups of nests, have been noted.

Certainly in the eastern lowlands herons are much fewer than one would like them to be.

Those who stock streams and lochs with trout might not agree.

Yet it has to be remembered that although herons take trout, they also capture many eels; and eels can do a lot of damage to trout in their early stages.

Herons also feed on frogs, rats, mice and even adders.

I can tell of one attacking and killing a stoat, and for all the bravery of the stoat, it had no answer to the stabbing blows of that spear-like bill.

At this nesting-time herons resort to trees, but this is by necessity and not by choice.

The bird is not well suited for life in the tree-tops, and looks awkward perching among the high branches.

Formerly these birds nested in reed-beds, and even today, in the Western Highlands, they still nest at ground level on rocky islets.

If you can spot a heron at his fishing before he sees you (which is not easy) you'll find that his methods vary.

Sometimes he goes "guddling" under banks and stones.

At tidal estuaries he stalks his prey, advancing step by step with neck craned forward and beak pointing down at the ready.

But generally the grey fisher stands patiently in the reedy shallows, waiting for fish to swim towards him.

This they do readily enough.

How could they see any cause for alarm in two stick-like legs, and plumes that wave in the wind like willow foliage?

Visit a heronry at this time of year and you'll find it a place of noise and bustle, with the birds keeping up a babel of barking and screaming, with bouts of beak-snapping thrown in, and noises like the clashing of cymbals.

Pop-groups have nothing on a heronry when nesting is in full swing!

Heron

MY drawing shows Powskeenie ("Pool of Leaping") and the bridge that leads over the North Esk to Dalbrack. To find this very lovely part of Glenesk you must diverge to the left about a mile beyond Tarfside.

Why "Pool of Leaping"? The name Powskeenie comes from the Gaelic poll sginnidh, and indicates a salmon-loup, where ascending fish often show themselves in negotiating a small cascade and a stretch of rough water.

But people, too, had to "loup" here in crossing the river before the bridge was built, and in the old days they jumped from rock to rock, hoping (with luck) to arrive at the other side dry-shod.

But when the "Northie" came roaring down in spate after a thunderstorm in the hills of Glen Mark and Glen Lee they didn't loup – if they were wise, they stayed on their own side of the river.

Glenesk's birchwoods are at their best just now in their springtime freshness, and roadsides are gay with the blossom of rowan and wild-cherry.

In this blossom-time the hawthorn is often overlooked, yet this is the most beautiful of our native flowering trees. After all, the laburnum and the horse-chestnut, decorative though they be, are exotic colonists, but the hawthorn is a true native.

No doubt hawthorns grow best in sheltered places, but they adapt themselves to circumstances.

On the coast they are sheared and moulded by the sea-winds.

In rocky outcrops of the glen they crouch down in self-defence, defying the mountain gales to wrest a single twig from their knotted branches.

Nevertheless, wherever a hawthorn grows, it never fails to show a profusion of flowers.

The trouble with hawthorn is that it is seldom punctual. Like a staid grown-up it has dropped the custom of keeping its birthday.

Although called "may," that month is often past before a sprinkling of white pellets (like the relics of a hailstorm) appears on the hedgerows, and even then it takes a few more sunny days before the flowers unfold, and their garlands fill the roadsides and country lanes with drifts of fragrant snow.

But to return to Powskeenie and Dalbrack. This is the start of "the Priest's Road" – an ancient and historic track that strikes over the Clash of Wirren into Glen Lethnot.

At one time it was a route much frequented by harvesters and whisky smugglers, but it was named after the minister of Lochlee.

His parish extended from Glenesk to Glen Lethnot, and to keep in touch with all his parishioners "the priest" had to make many a crossing of this arduous route – a trudge of twelve miles, with a climb of 1500 feet. And the same back!

Obviously, a minister of these parts needed strength in his legs as well as his discourse!

Powskeenie, on the North Esk at Dalbrack

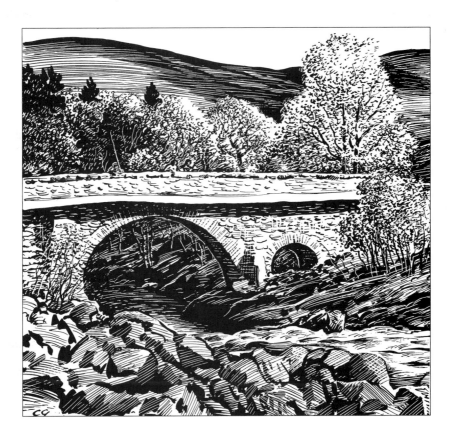

TILLYTOGHILLS – what a pleasant name for a farm! And what a fine farm toun this is, set with its back to the braes and its face to the Howe o' the Mearns.

One cannot but admire the farmhouse (it's in my sketch), the great trees that shelter it and the walled garden that John Milne has made a thing of beauty and a joy for ever.

Though the farm looks long established, John told me that the original Tillytoghills was sited farther up the hill than it is now.

At that time much of the lower ground lay as marshland and the rest of it was subject to periodic flooding.

The names of nearby farms, like Bogside, South Moss, Inch and Dryplaid, tell their own story.

Indeed, that was the way of it until Lord Adam Gordon (Commander-in-Chief of the forces in Scotland and proprietor of The Burn estate) set a batch of French prisoners, captured in the Napoleonic wars, to dig what came to be called "The Muckle Ditch."

You can still see this deep ditch cutting across the farmlands – not a thing of beauty in itself, but it drained a wide area and gave the farmers a chance to transform their sodden acres into good arable land.

May month brings a new flush of colour to the landscape of the Mearns, and the red broken earth contrasts quite startlingly with the freshening green of the pastures and the brere of the young wheat and barley.

It was good to see the birchwoods touched with green again, to see the gean tree blossom cradled on the wind, and wood anemones jostling and dancing under the trees.

Pale flowers too frail for winds so chill,
And with too fair a name…

But although that wind from the bare blue east still blew cold enough to mock away some of the sun's warmth, it had been shorn of much of its North Sea chill by the time it came over the fields of the Howe by way of Gourdon and Garvock and arrived at Tillytoghills.

The piping of oystercatchers and the "peesweep, weep-weep!" of lapwings were sounds that broke from the fields as I stood in John Milne's garden there and looked beyond his little orchard of apple trees to that well-loved landmark, the Johnstone Tower.

Tillytoghills, in the Mearns

June

ONE thing about camping in the Highlands in June – you get plenty of daylight. Among the hills night does not fall. What darkness there is comes welling up from the hollows and corries, but the sky retains its brightness and the afterglow of sunset burns on and on into the new day.

June is usually a fairly dry month, but as many campers know to their cost, it is not always so.

I can well remember getting permission with two companions to spend three weeks under canvas on a "painters' camp" holiday in Glen Affric. The mailcar-driver who helped to unload our gear said to us – "I hope you get good weather, whatever." If, instead, he had bestowed on us one of those long, all-embracing Highland curses, the weather could not have been worse.

It rained every day! Well, that is not quite true. One day it snowed, and there were other days when the rain that was ours by right just could not fall – it was carried horizontally past on the wings of the gale.

Our "painters' camp" didn't produce much in the way of art. Yet some wonderful effects were there – gleams of sunlight, cliffs of cloud and abysses of darkness, sudden glitters on the dark loch and river.

And after each rainy onslaught the mountain slopes and rugged pines were splendidly clear, with the birchwoods a dancing fairyland.

But the fickle weather's cantrips were all too transient for us. I felt it needed, not a brush, but an arrow to transfix these fugitive effects! One minute a corrie would be sunlit, azure in its shadows; next minute it was a liquid gulf, full of nothing but wind and rain!

"Ach well," said the head-keeper philosophically, "it is better to get it all over and done with." The trouble was, we couldn't stay that long!

However, with more experience, a less weighty sketching-kit, and an ability to seize upon an effect more quickly, I did manage to combine hill-climbing with watercolour painting.

Mountains like Liathach, Beinn Eighe and Beinn Damh (at Torridon) were great outdoor "studios," with a world of new colour and perspectives. Skye held further attractions, with Blaven my special favourite. Ben Hiant and Beinn na Seilg in Ardnamurchan were other delightful vantage points.

My drawing this week (from a painting I made on the summit-ridge of Beinn Eighe, "the file-edged peak") shows one of its nine "tops," the quartzite escarpment of Sgurr Ban.

One item of my sketching-kit often raised eyebrows, but I found it extremely useful.

It was a large and colourful golfing umbrella. On the hilltops even buzzards "mewed" with excitement and curiosity when they saw it, but it could temper the chilly mountain winds, and often allow a continuance of work during a hill-shower.

On one occasion, after crossing the hills from Torridon to Achnashellach via Coire Lair, I went and left it on the railway platform. But I got it back.

Next day, at Strathcarron, a railway guard called to me in a Highland accent – "Wass it you who left your parasol at Achnashellach?"

I had to confess it was I.

Sgurr Ban, Beinn Eighe

THE season of the young birds is upon us! We can hardly step out of doors without disturbing a family in feathers.

For townsfolk, it may be only a couple of young sparrows quivering their wings in the wake of their perky parent. But in the country you never know whom you may disturb.

At the grassy edge of a field I thought the earth had exploded under my feet. Then I recognised the cause. Two partridges were scurrying in a mad semi-circle in front of me – the hen bird quite near, the cock at a safer distance – both with wings drooping and cluttering furiously.

In a situation like this you must ca' canny. Don't move a step forward until you have scanned the ground, or you might well put your foot on a baby partridge or two crouching in the grass. You will probably begin to see others – one to the left, one to the right, one here, two there.

Step gingerly and pass on, leaving the partridge family to reassemble, with mutual congratulations on the success of their manoeuvre.

Alongside a stream you may catch a glimpse of a wild duck slipping behind the rank fringe of water plants. Go nearer and you find no trace of any wild duck whatever. The stream ripples on and the meadow-sweet and loosestrife sway in the summer breeze.

Then, suddenly, with a scurry over the water, appears – a lame duck!

It flaps along the water a few yards at a time and, if you don't know the ways of the wild duck, you will follow it for a hundred yards or more along the waterside, only to find that the broken wing has miraculously healed and the bird is perfectly able to fly back to the flotilla of fluffy brown and yellow ducklings lurking patiently under cover of the waterweeds. They are but a few days old, but wise with the instinct of centuries.

If you are near a farm, you may notice that there are now twice as many swallows as there were when they first arrived some weeks back.

And well there may be, for Nature's factory of bird life has been in full blast, turning out whole families of young swallows to every pair that fixed their nest to the beam of an old cowshed.

Swallows are not fussy about where, or at what height, they nest, as long as they have a roof over their head. I remember coming upon a swallows' nest at less than shoulder level in a derelict cottage at Chapelton.

I remember, too, an old relic of a shafted grocery van standing all alone and at a rakish angle on Kelly Moor near Carmyllie, when the moor was much more extensive than now.

How an ancient baker's van came to be out here, bearing the brunt of the wind on the heath, was a mystery I never solved. But swallows requisitioned it and it served as a nursery for many generations of their progeny.

Swallow at Nest

CARLINHEUGH Bay and Castlesea Bay – what wonderful places for wild flowers are the sea-meadows of these sheltered havens near Auchmithie!

When in full bloom the Meadow-Cranesbill with its handsome blue flowers can hardly go unnoticed. But the rather drastically named Bloody Cranesbill with its red-purple flowers is less easy to find.

It grows on a steep sunny bank under the red sandstone rocks of Carlinheugh (Witch Cliff), quite near a rock engraved with a sailing ship and the gloomy portals of the Dark Cave.

The Greater Knapweed, with its plumed rose-coloured flower-heads, also grows within sight and sound of the sea, and a white variety is worth searching for.

Thrift – also called the Sea Gilliflower – seems to delight in proving how little nourishment it requires, for it grows in the cracks of rocks just outwith the reach of the waves.

Sea-Rocket, however, prefers the sandy shore, and its flowers vary from lilac to white. The fruit is a little pod – a great favourite with greenfinches and other small birds.

Many of the seaside flowers are yellow – like Ragwort (its vegetation so often devoured by cinnabar-moth caterpillars), Hawkbit and Hawkweed, Toadflax, and Tormentil with its four small petals arranged like a Maltese cross.

Notable exceptions are Ragged Robin, a flower of marshy ground, and Sea Campion, which likes nothing better than a dry sunny ledge with a nice sea view.

Among the rocks, too, but growing in sheltered caves and shadowed crevices, one may find the Clustered Bell-flower and a variety of ferns.

Searching for wild flowers, it's a bit surprising to come upon a patch of potato plants in full bloom, and promising a good crop to follow.

It may be that this seaside vegetable plot was established by "The Hermit" – an old chap who once lived in a small cave nearby.

But more likely the potatoes were dumped over the cliff from the fields above, and took root 200 feet below.

My sketch shows Castlesea Bay – delightfully sheltered by the bold headland called Lud Castle, and accessible from the landward side by way of Lairick Den.

"Lairick"? That's the local version of laverock or lark – that sweet minstrel of the sky.

Castlesea Bay

HOW many hillwalkers of today can remember the early days of the Scottish Youth Hostels? Sydney Scroggie can, I know, and there are probably others who can think back to the first hostels – so much simpler than most of those today.

Some years ago, Stan Leckie – a member of the executive committee in those legendary days of the association – asked me if I could recall the old hostel in Glen Clova, the predecessor of Glendoll Lodge.

I certainly could. It was one of the wooden chalet type, and especially busy with hill-walkers at weekends, mainly from Dundee and Aberdeen. Sometimes not only the two-tier beds but the aisle between was needed to accommodate all the hostellers.

This building (officially opened by that stalwart Highland laird, the late Earl of Airlie) had a fine situation on a birchen knoll at Newbiggin, overlooking a loop of the South Esk.

The view of the upper glen, both from here and from nearby Caddam (as in my sketch) was truly magnificent.

Motherly Mrs Harper was warden at this hostel, and she greeted all in her own homely fashion.

In those days, every hosteller made a point of doing some task before leaving. It might be cleaning the windows, or redding up the food cubicles.

One morning I noticed an adult hosteller and his two sons busily scrubbing out the lavatory. He told me it was a job most people avoided at the hostels, so he and his sons took upon themselves to do it.

On another occasion, two girl students scrubbed the trestle dining-table, then left it resplendent with a bouquet of wild flowers.

One night, when everyone seemed to be asleep, a young chap came stealthily alongside my bed and whispered, "Colin, there's somebody round at the back stealing the bikes!"

I got up quietly, and the two of us tiptoed from the dormitory to the common-room, then out into the rainy darkness. And here was a family – father, mother and two small boys – utterly exhausted, and trying to find shelter in the bicycle shed rather than disturb the peace of the whole hostel.

They had walked from Braemar, never dreaming that "Jock's Road" entailed climbing to over 3000 feet, that the weather might worsen, or that the track might prove difficult to follow.

We brought them indoors, filched a few blankets off various sleepers' beds, and parked them out around the common-room stove. And in spite of all the morning bustle and clatter at breakfast-time, they still lay there sleeping until noon!

Midsummer days at Newbiggin were especially delightful. As each day ended, shadows welled up in the hollows of the hills, but there was no real darkness.

In the radiant sky there was but a slender bridge of shadow between the red lakes of sunset and dawn. On Ben Reid's burly shoulder, the afterglow of sunset gave way to the red fleece of sunrise.

The man who started the youth hostel movement was Egerton St John Catchpool, a lifelong Quaker and pacifist.

All youth hostellers should remember him.

Upper Glen Clova

July

IF you follow the Elliot Water from Arbirlot Mill through Cuthlie Den you eventually arrive at the gates of Paradise. This Paradise is a rough pasture alongside the burn, sheltered by woods and whinny braes. It's one of many unusual field-names hereabouts – like Fluthers, The Zeppelin, The College and Blue Breeks.

Field-names, like ordinary place-names, often carry hidden meaning.

Of those mentioned, The Zeppelin records bombs dropped in the first world war; The College refers to an ancient ecclesiastical building of which no trace remains. Fluthers was at one time subject to flooding.

Blue Breeks may have been Blue Riggs at one time, or even Bare Breeks, alluding to its former poor yield.

On a bank alongside the woods at Paradise I saw an unusual skirmish between a queen bumble-bee and a shrew-mouse.

The shrew had apparently been caught in the act of raiding the brood-comb within the nest, and had been stung for its trouble.

It was now squeaking and springing at its assailant, which kept swooping down with a deep, angry hum. At length the shrew darted away – no doubt to lie low and lick its wound till the anguish ceased.

These big queen bees – furry yellow and black – differ from hive bees quite a lot.

The queen, having survived the winter, makes her nest in a burrow. There she stores honey, and then proceeds to lay a few eggs.

She tends the young carefully through the grub and chrysalis stages, and they grow into workers. These now undertake the work of the hive, while the queen lays more eggs. But, unlike the sequestered queen of the hive, she still goes booming forth each day in search of honey.

Later in the summer, when her swarm is strong, she begins to lay drone-eggs and queen-eggs. These drones are not like the lazy, greedy spongers of the hive – they soon leave the nest to forage for themselves.

The new queens, too, are carefully prepared for their journey out into the world, and soon they fly away, never to return.

Her work done, the mother-queen forsakes the burrow. Her workers begin to die off, and she now spends the fleeting summer days among her favourite flowers.

But soon she will grow more and more listless and heavy with sleep.

And one day you or I may find her lying beside a blossom or in the grass. Still, she has lived her life to the full, and left a score of royal daughters to carry on the traditions of her race.

Shrew and Bumble-bee

IF you cross the majestic Tay at Dunkeld by that fine bridge designed by Telford, you'll see an old toll house standing on the far side. From it, a footpath leads down the right bank of the river towards Birnam.

It's a pleasant walk, and not one to be hurried over.

There are some fine vistas looking upstream (as in my sketch) towards a wooded island and the craggy hill called Craig-y-Barns.

Then, farther on, at Birnam, you come upon two very notable trees – a venerable oak and an equally ancient sycamore.

These are the remaining stalwarts of that famous Birnam Wood that enters so dramatically into Shakespeare's Macbeth.

The oak, with its immense horizontal beams and layered boughs, is very impressive.

And few trees in Britain can have so massive a trunk as this centuries-old sycamore growing by the banks of the Tay.

There are other famous trees in the Dunkeld district.

One is Niel Gow's oak, beneath which that most renowned of Scottish fiddlers used often to sit and compose a lively tune.

> Nae fabled wizard's wand I trow,
> Had e'er the magic art o' Gow,
> When wi' a wave he draws his bow
> Across his wondrous fiddle…

Miss E. M. Macintosh, of Dunkeld, showed me a reel-stand made specially for her by her uncle, Charles Macintosh (the naturalist and musician) from a fallen bough of this notable tree.

I was also told about the Hangman's Tree, where many a Highland outlaw paid the penalty for his misdeeds.

Then there's the Bummin' Tree, another sycamore, named from the hum of innumerable bees in its foliage at flowering time.

Not least, by any means, is a Douglas fir, one of many noble trees to be seen at The Hermitage – that is, in the wooded glen of the Braan, the Tay's turbulent tributary beyond Inver.

This Douglas-fir is believed to be the tallest tree in Britain.

It towers from the edge of a dark pool for 180 feet – about 30 feet higher than Dundee's Old Steeple!

The Douglas-fir has done well in Perthshire.

It was discovered in Northwest America by a Scot, Archibald Menzies.

Another Scot (the botanist David Douglas) sent the first seeds to this country in 1828.

The Hermitage (or "Ossian's Hall") is a pavilion set high on rocks overlooking one of the Braan's most impressive waterfalls.

It was originally built in 1758 for the eldest son of Lord George Murray, Prince Charles Edward Stewart's General in the '45 Rebellion.

In time this son became the third Duke of Atholl.

Notice all these traditional Scottish names – Menzies, Douglas, Stewart, Murray.

What a wonderful county Perthshire is for noble trees, castles and old Scottish family names!

As Francis Bacon once wrote: "It is a reverent thing to see an ancient castle or building not in decay, or to see a fair timber tree sound and perfect; how much more to behold an ancient family which hath stood against the waves and weathers of time."

The Tay at Dunkeld

BRANDY Cave, Rum Ness, the Forbidden Cave, Dickmont's Den, Cove Ha'en – the very names "smell" of smugglers!

There is no sign now of the old fisher huts that stood above the storm beach at Cove Ha'en (two miles from Arbroath), but the "fishermen" who dwelt here were probably more concerned with cargoes brought over the North Sea from the Netherlands than on their legitimate harvest of haddies and codlins.

For them the Masons' Cave served as a boathouse and hide-out long before the Freemasons of "St Tain's" made their St John's Day processions, and held their secret rites in its gloomy interior.

Dickmont's Den, too, has its smugglers' cave, with an entrance facing seawards, and a handy "back door" leading inland.

If you look down at one point of the clifftop path you can see the Deil's E'en (sometimes called the Cat's E'en) glinting from the darkness of this cavern.

Many of the frightening tales connected with the caves were probably circulated by the smugglers themselves to keep folk away.

The Forbidden Cave (on the far side of Carlinheugh Head) had all sorts of weird associations, as well as a tale of an old-time bagpipe player, lost and wandering in its depths.

The fact that this cave has a very small entrance subject to earth and rockfalls no doubt made it a place of fearsome imaginings.

Prail Castle (once called Garecock Head), Lud Castle, the Red Head – these majestic headlands are more associated with seabirds than with smugglers.

Cliff-tenements, they might be called, or multi-storeys, housing an extraordinary variety of sea-fowl.

Puffins, guillemots, razorbills, eiders, shags, rock-doves, herring-gulls, kittiwakes, fulmars – they all find accommodation here.

The Red Head has served as an eyrie for many generations of those other freebooters of the coast, peregrine falcons.

I have often watched peregrines from the airy brow of this great rock.

A falcon will spend quite a time idling in the sea-winds, even allowing itself to be chivied aside by herring-gulls.

But when the hunting mood comes upon it, it sallies forth in purposeful flight.

A few flicks of the wings to gain speed and height, then zoom! it goes down to strike its quarry (usually a rock-dove) with its powerful talons.

The speed of this swoop is estimated at 180 m.p.h., and it makes a sound like the swish of a rocket.

Driftwood Cave (shown in my sketch) lives up to its name, and I have usually found a great pile of driftwood, along with a conglomeration of sea-rubbish, at its inner end.

A man told me that on one occasion he found a whole cartload of old potatoes!

No doubt they had been tipped over the cliff edge, and stowed away here (in smuggler fashion) by the omniverous sea.

Inside the Driftwood Cave (Arbroath cliffs)

IN Dundee recently I stood for a moment or two looking up at the Old Steeple, which towers up to 150 feet.

"What are you seeing up there?" a passer-by asked me.

"Well," I said, "in my mind's eye I'm seeing a waterfall in Wester Ross called the Fall of Glomach. It's twice as high as the Old Steeple plus another 50 feet."

In fact, the Fall of Glomach is reckoned to be the highest waterfall in this country, and is most easily approached from the head of Loch Long. But there is a waterfall near Kylesku (Sutherland) which is much higher, though it tends to fade somewhat in a dry spell.

This is Eas Mor Coul Aulin, and my drawing shows a small section of it lashing down its rock-face, with the head of Loch Cairnbawn in the background.

In the Highlands there are hundreds of waterfalls, but many of them, like that wanderer of the waterways, the otter, are here today and gone tomorrow.

A rainy night and every freshet comes down singing like a wren, and the slopes are all a-gleam with cascades. But within twenty-four hours they have lost their lustre, and unless there is more rain they will soon shrink away.

The slender cascade on Braeriach (Cairngorms) comes from springs called the Wells of Dee, and is less dependent on direct rain, making its first infant cry among the moss and granite-detritus at over 4000 feet. No river in this country has such a lofty beginning as the Aberdeenshire Dee.

And yet I remember a streamlet that rises on the summit-ridge of Ben Eighe, "the file-edged peak" near Loch Maree.

As a silver thread it falls sheer down the north face of Sgurr Ban, one of the mountain's nine peaks, to a rock-shelf with a dark pool.

This overspills into the seldom-visited Corrie nan Clach, "Corrie of the Stones." Farther down, other streams come to join it, and, like a mesh of silver cords flung over the slopes, they draw utter chaos into the form of a glen – Glen Grudie, leading down to Loch Maree.

Again, that fall tends to vanish in dry weather, but Reekie Linn, on the Isla, is not one of these. It is always impressive, bounding over a broken precipice for 100 feet into a cauldron of a pool as black as night. Farther down, at the Slug of Auchrannie, it leaps again into a gloomy cage of rocks, and then the waters race on to meet the Melgam below the crags of Airlie Castle, the "Bonnie Hoose" of the old song.

The trouble with many waterfalls is that they lie far away in inaccessible places. Yet the Falls of Acharn, not far from Killin (Loch Tay) are very beautiful, and well worth the small detour needed to reach them.

Up this way, too, is one of the finest fall-streams in all Scotland. This is a hill-burn that comes down to join the Tay at Aberfeldy.

To follow the path that leads from this pleasant Highland town into the woods of the den is to enter a whole succession of enchanted dells – secret magical places of sunlight and leaf-shadow, of rock and fern, and everywhere the sound and movement of falling waters.

The highest waterfall (Glen Coul)

August

CERES must be one of Fife's loveliest villages, and with the surrounding farmlands lying golden in August sunshine it was almost possible to believe it derived its name from Ceres, the Roman goddess of tillage and corn.

It didn't, however, and the stone carving that stands in the village centre represents not an ancient deity but a 16th century Provost. Thomas Buchanan was his name, and his squat, quaint figure was carved by one John Howe, of Saughtree.

From the "Auld Brig" and the famous Bow Butts (once the scene of archery contests and country fairs) I followed the burn down the pastoral valley that leads to Pitscottie.

It was good to see a fair-sized flock of lapwings flying over the fields. Sad to say, these birds seem to dwindle in number year by year.

Five roads converge at Pitscottie, and the one I took still followed the Ceres Burn, now nearing Dura Den.

"Beware of fallen rocks" motorists are warned in this long wooded ravine.

The reason is obvious, for here and there rocks tower over the roadway, and sandstone escarpments are by no means the most stable of rock formations.

These yellowish-hued rocks are worth a careful look for another reason. They are richly fossil-bearing, and many a geologist has travelled far to see and examine them.

I passed several bridges, and one of these, spanning the burn alongside a trim row of cottages, is shown in my sketch.

Several meal mills and flax mills were established in this area at one time, harnessing the burn to drive their machinery.

Near one of these disused mills I left the road to get a closer view of several waterfalls.

They were worth seeing – white water leaping in shafts of sunlight, mossy rocks glittering with spray, dark pools studded with foam and ringed with rising trout.

A den like this is a natural sanctuary for wild birds, and many species could be listed here.

A water-ousel specially interested me, for I was sure it was singing. This is a bird that sings right through the year, and yet is seldom heard.

The reason? Simply that its sweet song is seldom audible above the water noise.

At the foot of Dura Den a side-road climbs and twists its way to the graceful Kemback Church and Kemback School.

Higher still, as a footpath, it surmounts "Jenny's Brae" by a remarkably long flight of steps. Then it leads onward to the red-roofed cottages and upland smallholdings of Blebo Craigs.

This is a "scholars' roadie," used by the bairns coming over the hill from Blebo. Lucky scholars, with one of the pleasantest views in Fife spread before them every morning!

In Dura Den, Fife

GROUSE are fast fliers and, driven forward by the beaters, they may well reach the butts at 60 miles per hour, swerving and rocking from side to side. No wonder so many of them go whirring and skimming past without losing a feather!

Sometimes the driven grouse fly high, at other times so close to the heather as to be invisible till the last moment.

Former gamekeeper, Sandy Pringle of Lundie, once told me of this happening at a grouse shoot out that way. The grouse came over thick and fast – and so low that their wings were almost clipping the heather.

Lord Moyne's ghillie sized up the situation and startled those in the butts with a great shout: "Jeuk yer heids, yer dukes an' yer dukesses!" None of the guns knew what he meant but at least they instinctively ducked, and I need hardly add that the result of that drive was nil.

In the reign of King George V, when shooting from butts was at its most popular, the King himself was reckoned to be one of the best shots on the moors. His speed and accuracy with the gun were extraordinary.

He was less successful with the rifle among the crags and corries of the deer forest. A tale is told of His Majesty completely missing a fine stag, though the shot was a fairly easy one.

He was clearly annoyed and thrust the rifle into the hands of his head stalker. "Take that rifle away!" he said. "Never let me see it again."

The head stalker was unperturbed.

"There's naething wrang wi' the rifle, Your Majesty," he said.

"It was juist a damned bad shoat."

When I was a young lad, some of my chums and I used to go for a week at the beating. A hard job, for it entailed trudging for many miles each day over rough hill moorland, through bracken waist high and often soaking wet, crossing innumerable burns and peat-hags.

The weather, too, was not all that kind to us at times. I remember downpours of rain and such fusillades of hail that even the head keeper (not the most considerate of men) would shout to our wavering line – "Tak' shelter, lads!"

On the open moor, "shelter" meant cowering in a hollow and turning your collar up!

But we had a lot of fun, too, especially in our bothy in the evenings – singing the popular songs of the day, arguing and playing games of one sort or another.

Much time was, by necessity, spent in drying off stockings and boots, soaked in peaty water. Stockings were apt to be scorched by the stove and boot-leather came very near the cracking stage of no return. Dubbin and more dubbin was the only answer!

Altogether it was a salutary experience, but for many of us, including myself, it was a first introduction to the Highland hills, and in fine weather the views from the high ground were unforgettable.

At the beating

WADING in shallow tidal pools at the seaside may lack the excitement of bathing among breaking waves, but it has pleasant compensations. Not least, a re-introduction to that fish of character, the flounder or fluke.

What a curious feeling it is, for instance, when you put your foot on one, and feel it squirming in its efforts to skim away to safety!

Fisher-folk used to spear flounders, but this is a type of fishing that requires some dexterity of aim if you have any regard for your own toes! Perhaps it is better to leave the spearing to that bird with the spear-like bill, the heron.

Flounders are regarded as saltwater fish, but nevertheless they are quite adaptable – and adventurous. Not satisfied with sandy shores, some of them make their way far up rivers and streams – the Tay, the Eden, the Elliot, the South Esk.

Waterfalls halt their progress, as flat fish are not structurally built for high jumping like salmon. But on placid waters they will venture for miles – skimming into the unknown!

There is an old belief that a seawater fish put into fresh water (and vice versa) will die. This is not always the case and trout, for instance, that live in tidal estuaries are changing from fresh to salt water every few hours.

In the tidal reaches of Lunan Water at Lunan Bay (the mouth of this stream is the subject of my sketch) I watched an angler catch, first, a brown trout and then a flounder immediately after.

Had he been properly equipped he might even have added a stickleback to this mixed bag, for that is another fish quite at home in fresh or salt water.

Salmon feed in the sea, but spawn in the fresh water of our rivers. Eels live and grow in our rivers, but descend to the sea as mature fish, and make an epic sea journey to spawn in the South Atlantic.

The rainbow-trout is something of a mystery. A freshwater fish, it has nevertheless a strange liking for salt water. Given the opportunity – afforded, say, by a faulty sluice-gate, or an overflow in rainy weather – the rainbow will make with all haste for the coast and the sea.

Once there, its characteristic tints begin to disappear, and soon the fish becomes a plain silver-grey.

So stock your angling lochs and reservoirs with rainbow-trout if you will. But remember, they will migrate if they can find a way.

And once in the briny, these fish show no inclination to return!

At Lunan Bay

RUINED Forter Castle – up for sale recently – was half hidden in mist and rain the last time I passed it in upper Glen Isla. Castles built so near the Grampians are liable to get some wicked weather!

I remember John Davidson, shepherd at Forter, telling me they often had a hundred days of snow lying there over the winter months. Even in May the slopes of the higher hills could still be heavily snow-patched.

This year, of course, snow fell unashamedly in June and the chill of late August rain suggested that more snow would soon be on the way!

Back in the 17th century the hill-farmers up this way suffered heavy losses, not as a result of bad weather but at the hand of the caterans, those wild men of the hills who were ever liable to swoop down and steal the glensmen's cattle – aye, and often to burn and slay!

Forter in those unruly days was a stronghold in the midst of the hill-farms.

It was then a "bonnie house" of the Lords of Airlie, and it was probably from its walls that the brave Lady Airlie defied the "fause Argyll," who came with orders to "ding doon" the great Castle of Airlie and this smaller castle of the upper glen.

> *Argyll has ta'en five hunder o' his men,*
> *Five hunder o' his men and mairly*
> *And he's awa' by yon green shaw*
> *To plunder the Bonnie Hoose o' Airly.*

It is difficult to fix on the exact source of the Isla. It has several headstreams, and you can't (as at the Wells of Dee in the Cairngorms) point to water welling up in a gravelly hollow and say – "Here is the birthplace of the river."

Nevertheless, the Isla's streamlets rise at 3100 feet in surroundings not unlike those of the Royal Dee. The crest of Lochnagar soars up to the north-east, and the bare summit of Glas Maol is near at hand to the south-west.

Leaving the stony, windswept plateaux, the Isla is still an unnamed river and assumes its name only when those two hill-waters, the Red Burn and the Glashie, meet at The Shielin.

The building that inspired this name has long since gone but the view remains, with its noble vistas of the two mountain recesses, Caenlochan and Canness.

On a bright day of sun and flying clouds, I have seen the rocks of Caderg, the Ewe Howes and Monega become an arabesque of sunshine and shadow, and after heavy rain-showers the burns hold the crags in a mesh of silver cords.

A fine stream, the Isla. Below Forter Castle it flows on pleasantly in ripple and race through the little fields and pastures of its glen. It's a stream that has "rugged at the hert" of many an exile.

> *Winding flows the Cam,*
> *But it's no my ain loved Isla;*
> *Rosy decked the meads,*
> *But they're no like dear Glen Isla!*

Forter Castle, Glen Isla

September

IN September, with the earlier fall of dusk and darkness, the gentle stars of summer give way to the brighter panoply of autumn, as if to remind us that the wheel of the seasons keeps turning.

Outwith the distraction of street lighting, it is difficult to look up at this starry firmament without a feeling of awe. Astronomers calculate that the Milky Way, the hazy band that stretches across the deeps of the sky, contains over 100,000 million stars. How tiny one can feel in comparison with so vast a universe!

I am no astronomer, but at least I can always recognise the constellation of the Plough and the steadfast Pole Star. "Follow the handle of the Plough," I was told as a boy, "and you'll find the Herdsman, with a bright star called Arcturus."

Taurus the Bull ranges nearer the horizon's rim, and I can usually pick out the Pleiades or Seven Sisters, even if I can never see more than six!

Perseus, Andromeda and Pegasus all have their place in a memorable legend of the skies, and probably they have changed very little, if at all, since the days of Ancient Greece.

Though they have no interest in Greek mythology, many wild creatures prefer, for safety's sake, to move around by starlight rather than by sunlight.

Foxes, for instance, are well aware that every man's hand is turned against them, and they go a-hunting mainly after sunset.

Bats and owls are more naturally nocturnal, though they are mostly out and about in the early part of the night, and again at sunrise.

Otters, too, become active at dusk, and anglers fishing late for sea trout may occasionally catch a glimpse of one silhouetted against a patch of moonlit water. But more often this gypsy of the waterways slips silently and unobtrusively from pool to pool.

For that matter, fish also move long distances after the fall of dark. Fishing at night in time of low water (not this year!), I've often heard the splash of salmon surmounting the shallows from one pool to another.

In daylight their dorsal fins and broad backs would be seen out of the water, and obviously they feel safer travelling by night.

Family groups of roe deer will sometimes be encountered in broad daylight, browsing peacefully high up among the hills, but as a rule they delay venturing from their woodland cover until that quiet interlude "atween the gloamin' and the mirk."

The badger, an old true resident of this country, seldom stirs or looks out from his sett by day. A lover of the starlight and the moonlit glades, he has always worked the night shift, and prefers it that way.

In his sober black, white and grey, he matches his nocturnal paths – "the moon of centuries has silvered him."

Badger

IT was that notable climber, Professor Norman Collie, who really gave substance to the old legend of the Big Grey Man (Fear Liath Mhor) of Ben Macdhui, when he told a gathering of fellow-climbers of hearing slow and heavy footsteps following him in the mist-enshrouded Cairngorms.

But mist can bring an eeriness and an element of fantasy to any hills. The Lake Poet, Wordsworth, must have experienced similar feelings of disquiet when he wrote –

> I heard among the solitary hills
> Low breathings coming after me, and sounds
> Of indistinguishable motion, steps
> Almost as silent as the turf they trod.

I felt this eeriness in crossing the tarn-strewn Moor of Rossie, to the south of Farnell.

With the fields and farms of the strath and all landmarks hidden, a familiar landscape had now changed to a strange world of its own – grey, neutral, silent and unknown. Contacts with everyday life seemed suddenly to have grown alarmingly tenuous.

I trudged on – everything sodden, the air like muslin, the breath of the wind cold and wet. Not a sound but my own footsteps as I bruised dark tracks through the heather and grass.

Mist can be hallucinating in its effects. Everything is magnified.

A peewit rising from the marshes looked as broad-winged as a heron. A hillock near Nicholl's Loch loomed up like a mountain, a bush like a tree.

Whinny thickets were furtive apparitions that moved and vanished in the spectral air.

The disc of the sun appeared, but only for a moment as it went weaving its way through the mist. Moorland tarns emerged as white sheeted spectres, and pine-trees towered up like phantoms of the fog.

The old mounth roads over the Grampians must have been just as difficult to follow in mist as in snow.

When snowstorms obliterated the track, then standing-stones could be helpful. For instance, the Fir Mounth (north of Tarfside, Glenesk) suggests in its name that it had at least one "fear-breige" (or false-man) set up usefully on the skyline.

But in mist, this aid to direction would be useless, and with deer-tracks crossing the true route, a traveller deprived of his customary landmarks could well be led astray.

Even today, when most hill-walkers can use a compass, there are some who tackle Jock's Road (Glen Doll) and descend by Loch Esk and Bachnagairn, instead of Loch Callater and Glen Clunie, and find themselves back where they started!

Nevertheless, bewildering though they be, the effects of mist can also be enchantingly lovely. Our hills would never be the same without mist weaving its way among the crags and corries.

Mist softens the outline of trees, and casts a spell of romance over our Western Isles. And at sunrise, who can deny the beauty of the morning mist that lies like a veil over the land?

Pines in mist

WHEN, five centuries ago, David de Barkeley of Mathers was outlawed by King James I for taking part in a despicable conspiracy, he decided he would be better to find a safer refuge. So he made for the St Cyrus coast, and proceeded to:

Buyld a lordlie kaim / All onne the stonie rock,
Which mote defie the sovereign's arms / And eke the tampest's shok.

Well, whether or not this medieval stronghold proved inaccessible then, it is certainly inaccessible now – a veritable cliff-hanger, ready to fall prey to the hungry waves. You can see what remains of this Kaim of Mathers at the north end of the beach at St Cyrus (or "St Seerus"), that attractive village beyond Montrose.

Like many other folk, I never take the seaward route through St Cyrus without halting at the head of the path leading down to the foreshore. It's a marvellous viewpoint, with these immaculate sands and rocky outcrops far below, with rugged cliffs sheltering the bay and a vast expanse of sea beyond.

Lucky St Cyrus folk, to have a seascape of such wonder so close at hand!

The sands, when you reach them, are delightful to explore. My sketch shows the outcrops of rock – some of them fantastic in shape including one like a huge "tappit hen" – and all left clean and sparkling by the receding tide.

The St Cyrus Nature Reserve stretches westwards for four miles along the coast to the mouth of the North Esk and a wide tract of deserted channel and salt marsh. It is an area quite remarkable both for its bird and plant life.

In autumn the coastal traffic of birds moving southwards is very heavy, and many wading birds and a colourful variety of ducks pause here to feed and rest in the tidal reaches.

It was here, when I was a young lad, that I first realised that not all ducks said "Quack!" Several handsome pintails, on rising, astonished me with a fair sample of their melodious flute-like alarm-call.

The plant life of the saltings, and of the slopes of the inland heughs, is extremely rich and varied. I was told that field-botanists have noted nearly 200 different flowering plants on these slopes, and in the whole reserve there are at least 300. And apparently this is the most northerly "station" for quite a number of the wild plants found growing here.

In September the nesting season is virtually over, though it is often the ninth month before young fulmars make their first flight to the seas. Young eiders, too, are not always in a hurry to begin their life on the ocean wave.

At the foot of the heights called "The Steeples" there is a lonely little kirkyard, and in a corner of it is "Beattie's Grave."

George Beattie was a Montrose lawyer, but came to be better known in his day as a local poet. He ended his own life here, describing himself as a broken-hearted lover, and his grave adds a touch of romance to the sough of the wind and the voice of the sea.

St Cyrus Beach

THE grain harvest is mainly past, and many a field now lies in stubble. Crimson haws and scarlet hips ripen in the hedgerows, and already autumn has laid a fiery finger on the leaves. Mornings grow noticeably chillier, and white mists gather on the links and marshes at sunset.

Yet, as this year, September often brings a spell of quiet sunny weather, when the whole countryside lies in a sea-like calm – a peace of fulfilment.

Migrant birds seem sweir to go. They linger till the north wind reminds them that summer is past. Some later-nesting birds, like house-martins, are still feeding young in their nests, and will delay their departure until these late broods are strong on the wing before beginning their long journey.

Birds are the great migrants, covering hundreds of miles from their nesting places to ensure for their species a better chance of survival.

Yet some animals and insects are also seized with the same seasonal restlessness, and their journeys (though more limited) are made with similar purpose.

But there are also the stay-at-homes – birds (like ptarmigan, that thole wintry weather on our highest hills); animals (like hedgehogs, which hibernate through the colder months); and insects (like queen bumble-bees, that lie in some sheltered crevice and dream of springtime flowers).

In the meantime, however, the stubbles of early autumn can provide a time of feasting. Gulls, rooks, starlings, jackdaws and partridges all feed on the fallen grain. So do some of the smaller fry – greenfinches, chaffinches, bank-voles and wood-mice.

The furry folk wisely store food for the hungry months, unlike the birds.

In these days of streamlined farming methods, the autumn feast of the stubble does not last. When fields lay in stubble well into winter they formed a larder for many wintering birds such as fieldfares, redwings, snow-buntings and bramblings.

But the bare ploughlands that form the biggest part of our winter landscape nowadays must seem little more than a sodden or frozen waste to hungry birds.

The wood-pigeon can turn to many types of food – acorns, beech-nuts, elderberries, hips and haws, leaves of clover and marsh-marigold, turnip-tops, seed-pods of the dog-violet, snails and slugs. Feeding their young on pre-digested "pigeon's milk," the cushie-doo can raise a family any month of the year – and some of them do!

Wood-pigeon at nest

October

NOWADAYS you must go far into the Grampian glens to hear the autumnal "roaring of the stags." Yet, centuries ago, the same sound might well have been heard in many parts of the Lowlands.

Less than 150 years ago red deer still frequented the Forest Moor near Forfar, and large herds roamed freely over that magnificent tract of rolling moorland called the Forest of Alyth.

Remains of red deer have also been dug up from time to time in the Carse of Gowrie, at Tents Muir and on the links of Monifieth and Barry.

In fact, the name Monifieth is generally accepted to mean "the moor of the deer," and it may well be that men of Tayside chased the red deer and followed the roe long before they chased the "wee white ba' " over these links and dunes.

Roe deer still inhabit many Lowland woods, but the red deer have survived only by withdrawing to the wind-swept "forests" of the hilltop mosses and corries.

Many people think that deer forests are fenced, but few are, and for very good reasons. To erect 8-foot fencing over miles of rugged hill ground would be a very expensive undertaking.

And what good would it do? Falling snow soon nullifies the height of a fence, and, backed by the mountain gales, drifting snow is only too liable to cover it!

At the time of "the roaring," the red stag (normally a quiet and peaceable beast) becomes truculent and assertive, noisily "belling" his challenge to other stags or calling to the hinds.

This warlike attitude, however, lasts only through the breeding season. With the fall of the antlers in early spring, the most belligerent of stags soon quietens down.

With other stags he separates from the hinds, and makes for the solitude of the hill mosses. There he grazes in friendly fashion with stags he had outfought but a few months earlier – possibly with the very animal that deprived him of his retinue of hinds.

But if the stags spend their summer on the best of terms, the same cannot be said of the hinds. They are very quarrelsome, and frequently fight amongst themselves, rising on their hind legs and "boxing" with their forefeet.

Scotland's red deer are not particularly keen of sight, but deer stalkers maintain they have "the keenest nose in Europe."

My old friend, stalker Allan Cameron, of Moulzie, used to say "you can deceive a stag by his eye but not by his nose."

If the wind is in their favour red deer can detect a human being a mile away!

Red-deer stag roaring

I SING the Sidlaws! They neither reach such heights as the Ochils nor share with the Grampians their wild crags and corries. But for pleasurable hill-walking and entrancing views these moory slopes of the "Sooth Hills" come into their own.

Even a low-level walk along the base of the hills can be quite impressive.

On this autumn day my road led from Abernyte by way of Balloleys and the Lang Man's Grave to Bandirran.

And on the way, Gask Hill, King's Seat, Black Hill and Hill of Dunsinane all took their turn in sunshine and in shadow.

North of Stockmuir (which once had its ring of standing stones) I could see that strange little cone-shaped hill that rises under the rugged frown of the Auld Man o' Gask.

This is a hillock of history, well endowed with names.

You may, if you please, call it the Round Law, the Whirley Law, the Glenny Law, or even The Holmes.

In ancient times this was a religious site and seat of judgement.

Even today four parishes – Abernyte, Longforgan, Cargill and Kettins all meet on this dark, mysterious hillock.

But all this district is steeped in folk lore. Fairies used to haunt the hilltop howes and hollows of Black Hill, and on summer eves, so it is said, they descended to the dewy meadows to dance at a spot called Fairygreen.

In contrast, the Giant's Leap is a craggy, jackdaw-haunted gap between Black Hill and Macbeth's Castle.

Awesome even in sunlight, in misty weather it becomes a solitary frightening place of rocky phantoms that move and vanish in the spectral grey.

I once asked old Mrs Murdie, who lived for many years at The Holmes, if she wasn't frightened staying there among fairies and giants and witches and Lang Men.

But she just laughed, and said she'd never met anyone "mair frightenin' than hersel'."

Macbeth's Castle, on Hill of Dunsinane, was never a building of turrets and crowstepped gables.

It was a vitrified fort or "dun," and its layout of ditch and rampart can still be traced on this airy summit.

The Lang Man's Grave lies not on the hill, but by the dykeside.

But who the Lang Man was, nobody knows.

He may have been a leader slain at the storming of Macbeth's Castle and sent hurtling down the rocks and stone-shoots of Black Hill.

My sketch shows the stony face of this escarpment, and from this viewpoint a road strikes north over the quarried moor to the sheltered nooks and woods of Collace.

It was at the charming Kirkton of Collace that Andrew Bonar, one-time minister of this parish, met a local farmer one morning.

"Ye'll be gaun tae Pairth the day, Mister Bonar?"

"No!" came the unexpected reply. "I'm going to Jerusalem."

And it was quite true, for the young minister had been chosen by the General Assembly to go on a fact-finding mission to the Holy Land!

Black Hill of Dunsinane

WHEN, at the west end of Crombie Loch, I sent a cock-pheasant rocketing up from my feet, he rose with such a whirr and clamour the windmill at nearby Hairy Nicoll's cottage must surely have doubled its velocity!

Pheasants are strange birds – a mixture of extrovert and introvert. Normally they prefer to lie low rather than fly, and despite rearing and domestication they are shy and secretive.

When a pheasant does choose to fly, it rises almost vertically, using its twenty-inch-long tail as a stabiliser.

But, at a pheasant-shoot (as gamekeepers well know), many a wily cock-pheasant is expert at hiding himself away, and never faces the guns at all. Once the shoot is over, however, out he struts in all his oriental splendour, as if he knew in his pride (and would have us know as well) that his illustrious ancestors came over with the Romans, and that they had acquired extensive territories in this country as far back as Norman times.

Many pheasants enjoy an easy life, well fed on maize etc., and an abundance of food and protection from enemies lead to abnormal sizes and weights. Normally, a cock-pheasant weighs from 3 to 3½ lb., while a hen-pheasant averages between 2 and 2½ lb., but there are great variations.

Many pheasants live wild, and have no truck with gamekeepers or rearing-pens. Even then, they have plenty to eat, and their choice ranges widely from grain to grasshoppers, from slugs to strawberries, from worms to weed-seeds.

In fact, the contents of a pheasant's crop are often astonishing. On examination one bird had eaten 24 hazelnuts, another 37 acorns. Another had swallowed 48 snails in their shells. Still another had devoured 440 "leather-jackets" (larvae of the daddy-longlegs), and one was found to contain 725 wireworms!

No one can deny that the pheasant has a hearty appetite!

A constant crowing of pheasants is said to foretell rain, and it is believed that pheasants are quick to detect a distant rumble of thunder, and give a noisy warning.

But why, at dusk, the cock-pheasant has to tell the world in his lordly way that he is now retiring to roost is rather puzzling, for this boastful crowing has proved fatal to many a fine bird. Many a natural predator – and many a poacher – have marked the roosting-tree, and put that knowledge to good use "on a shiny night in the season of the year."

I find it difficult to figure the pheasant's call – "korr-kok!" is fairly near it. But I have known several keepers who could give a rendering very like the real thing. Perhaps not quite so realistically, however, as they could "do" the squeal of a rabbit in distress, the bark of a fox, or best of all the harsh "kwaarp, kwaarp" of a carrion-crow!

Cock-pheasant

GHOSTS are prone to walk at this time of year, and our part of Scotland has more than its fair share.

There is the White Lady at Kilspindie, said to be seen flitting through the trees on moonlit nights, and the Grey Lady of The Guynd, who sobs ever so sadly as she crosses the starlit glades.

A lame ghost, probably that of Cardinal Beaton, has for long limped up and down a stone stair at Ethie Castle looking for a secret room.

And poor Jock Barefut, hanged on a Spanish chestnut tree at the old castle of Finavon, may still be seen wandering around all that remains of this stronghold of Earl Beardie, the Tiger Earl.

Glamis is famous for its ghosts and there is "The Ghaist o' Fern Den" – a fearsome customer this, despite his good deeds. Kellie Castle, too (shown in my sketch) once had its ghost.

As for witches, Arbroath Cliffs have their Carlinheugh (or Witch Cliff) looming over the Dark and Forbidden Caves; and Carlin Maggie, turned to stone by the Devil, still stands on the windy heights of the Lomonds, above the hollow rocks of Glenvale.

I remember the late John Angus (author of that strange novel, "The Sheltering Pine") telling me that he once saw what he took to be a ghost on a country road.

He was hurrying along on this clear frosty night when suddenly a grey form rose above the drystone-dyke.

It faded away in the still keen air, then loomed up again in an awesome way! John got a proper scare, till he realised it was "a coo's braith" rising from a beast behind the dyke!

But some accounts of ghosts are less amusing. I have notes concerning several apparitions seen over the years at Kinnoull, Perth, and these are strange, puzzling and, indeed, disquieting encounters.

A ghost whose presence was not seen, but felt, came the way of a man walking from Tullybaccart to Dron by means of the old track over Redmyre Moor.

Halfway there he had a strong feeling that someone was walking alongside him, and he had this "companion" for some time.

I was able to tell him something he didn't know – that this ancient track is called the Priest's Road, and was used by monks walking from the Abbey of Coupar (Angus) to Dron Chapel, built in the days of Malcolm the Maiden, and still standing in part. Perhaps one of the brethren was revisiting his old haunts and glad of a little company!

The only ghost I ever encountered myself was a motor lorry.

This is perfectly true. The lorry appeared on the road ahead of me when I was walking south over the moor from Sconser Lodge in Skye. The road was open and undulating and the lorry went into a dip as it drew near. I drew into the verge to let it pass.

But it didn't pass, and I never saw it again!

I thought it rather mysterious, but discussed it only with my wife.

In fact, I had more or less forgotten the incident when I happened to read an article about Skye, some years later, in the "Scots Magazine."

In it, the author (Seton Gordon) mentioned a "Phantom Lorry" which had been seen by a number of people – on this same stretch of road!

Kellie Castle, near Arbirlot

November

November's sky is chill and drear,
November's leaf is red and sere.

SO wrote Sir Walter Scott on the first page of Marmion. But November's skies are not always so. Often the rainy nimbus will drift away, leaving a sky bugle-blue and clear and in the slanting autumn sunlight the fields and woods, the lochs and hills were never more beautiful.

At one time visiting the hills and glens was almost wholly a summer exploit. But nowadays people are out on the hills all the year round and one has only to visit the popular glens or look at magazines devoted to climbing, skiing and hill-walking to see how these sports have caught on.

It is interesting to recollect that "The Climber" (one of the first magazines of this sort) started in a very modest way in Dundee and was edited for a time by R. R. Butchart at 2 Gardner Street. I remember presenting the editor with a spare ice-axe I had when he called to see me.

The lesser glens of the Braes of Angus have always appealed to me – especially Glen Quiech.

It's not a glen for cars, but interesting to explore on foot. North of Memus and Dykend the Glen Quiech road passes a lochan framed in larch then climbs to Horniehaugh ("Devil's Meadow") and a dark chasm of fir called Doulie Den.

Beyond Scalywell, the picturesque cottage in my sketch, the road soon deteriorates into a stony, waterlogged track. It climbs over a moory stretch then descends to a "sleeper brig" over the White Water, a small but lively burn.

Here stands Shallgreen, once a sheep farm, and beyond it on a green slope lies a rickle of mossy stones known as "The College." These stones are mindful of another "College" at Arbirlot, near Arbroath, connected in its day with Arbroath Abbey.

It seems odd that the Arbirlot "College" has alongside it a habitation called Palace Green, while "The College" in Glen Quiech has its Shallgreen. In Gaelic-derived placenames green or grian refers not to colour but to the sun.

From Shallgreen a grassy track leads upstream to Buckies, set under two hills with rather awesome names – Auld Darkney and Naked Tam. On the higher ground, too, is Anniegathel – an extraordinary name, probably referring in its Gaelic form to a ford and some ploughed land.

On the west side of the glen, on the lower slopes of Ben Scravie, lies the site of Rashiebog – once the "beinly winsome hame" of Dauvit Ogilvy – crofter, philosopher and maker of illicit whisky.

Dauvit built his own cottage, steadings, dykes, ploughs and carts. The cart ropes were made from his horses' tails.

Implements and animals lasted a long time at Rashiebog. Bell, a piebald mare, lived for 33 years and her foal for 28. When the foal died Dauvit said he "would hae thocht naething aboot it had it been an auld baest."

What a wonderful little glen this is, with its Horniehaugh and its Doulie Den, its Scalywell and its Rashiebog – and not forgetting Auld Darkney and the bare slopes of Naked Tam!

A picturesque cottage in Glen Quiech, Angus

SPEAK about fan mail! Some time ago I had a whole batch of letters from the scholars of a country school.

One little girl wrote – "When my father is ploughing, the gulls come after the plough, and I hope you will come, too."

November brings ploughing time. And over by Tullybaccart I couldn't resist stopping to watch a tractor-plough at work, once more changing the stubble of a harvest that is past to furrows of moist brown loam.

It's a sight that gives satisfaction – a thing in itself wholesome and beautiful.

Today, of course, ploughing is mainly mechanised, and handling a tractor-plough looks easier than steering a horse-plough.

But though it demands less physical effort, it needs skill and experience if it is to be done well.

There is no use lamenting the advent of the machine.

But no one would deny that there were few more beautiful scenes in country life than a field of ploughland with two or three teams of horses at work – Clydesdale or Shire, dappled Percheron or Suffolk Punch, with necks arched, muscles rippling, manes blowing in the wind, and always a cloud of gulls gleaming in their wake.

To the north-west, under skies tossed and wild, lay Strathmore, with its mosaic of field and farmland, sunlit strips of trees and belts of shaded country.

Inevitably, I found my eyes ranging beyond the Great Strath to the wintry Grampians, deep in snow.

Yet, in the farmlands, the pink-brown broken earth was beginning to show again as the ploughing went forward, as if eager to repay the labour and care bestowed upon it.

It is an old land this, a land full of character, with its sturdy cottages of stone and roughcast harling, its drystane dykes, its farmsteads that gleam among their trees.

Here are fields well tilled, not a yard wasted, ploughed to the very edge, the shape of woodlands kept within strict bounds.

It's a contemporary farming landscape, with its mechanised implements and tractor-ploughs. And yet, there is tradition behind it all.

Every farm, every hillock has its ancient associations, and the farmer of today knows full well that not only his hands but the hands of many generations shaped these fields that are now in his keeping.

Moreover, the land itself is a good land – some say it is the finest farming country in the world.

And it, in its own way, has shaped the character and mould of the folk who have lived in it, called it home, and worked out their tenure with its sun and cloud, rain and snow.

View from Tullybaccart

A tree's a leerie kind o' loon,
Weel happit in his emerant goun
Thru the saft simmer days;
But, fegs, whan baes are in the fauld,
An' burds are chitterin' wi' the cauld,
He coosts aff a' his claise.

SO wrote that lovable Perth poet William Soutar in his Seeds in the Wind – a book of poems in Scots for children, for which I once had the pleasure of doing 40 illustrations. A collector's piece nowadays!

The "daft trees" were certainly "coostin' aff their claise" the time I went to see the Den of Alyth. A high wind roared in the treetops and sent the leaves flying – gold and saffron from birch and rowan, blood-red from the gean, russet from oak and sycamore. A great gust struck the larches and scattered their needles like golden rain. The burn, half choked with leafy detritus, flowed darkly and silently. A famous burn, nevertheless, for soon it passes under Alyth's "packhorse brig" and becomes a feature of this delightful little Perthshire town.

I can never pass this centuries-old bridge without looking for trout in the pool below. One winter day there were none. And no wonder! The burn was chock-full of ice floes, released from upstream by a rapid thaw after a spell of hard frost. Beyond the bridge lies Toutie Street – thus quaintly named after the herdsman who used to "tout" his horn as he led the common herd of cows uphill to graze on the pastures. An interesting link with olden times.

But to return to the autumn woods. A smallish tree seldom mentioned is the bird-cherry. It's lovely in spring with its racemes of white flowers and although the little black fruits are of no consequence to any creatures bigger than birds and fieldmice, it joins with another small tree, the field-maple, in lighting a flame of colour in autumn.

An Edinburgh gardener, Ian Drummond, told me that the oldest tree he ever helped to fell was a beech in a private avenue near Water of Leith. It was 32 feet around the trunk and eight feet in diameter. From its rings it appeared to be over 400 years old. A wonderful tree!

Ian also mentioned some very elderly laburnums. I remember three of these – no doubt beautiful in their youthful days – that stood like three old crones at Monifieth Grange. Short of stature, but of massive girth, they were no doubt as old as the ancient Castle of Grange, long since gone.

The Auld Brig, Alyth

DWELLERS on the margins of continents! Many of these wading birds to be seen just now on the shores of the Firth of Tay must have travelled hundreds of miles – and they will travel thousands more in the course of their lives.

Duck, too, of various sorts find respite from stormy weather in the comparatively quiet waters of the Tay estuary. There is often an enormous raft of eiders at the mouth of the river at this time of year.

Heavy birds, built to stand the buffetings of heavy seas, these "dunters" are nevertheless fast fliers and can overtake most other birds of the foreshore.

At the sheltered tidal basin of the lordly Tay's last tributary, the humble Buddon Burn, I noticed quite a variety of passage migrants – dunlin, noisy redshanks and sandpipers that went flickering away over the shallows.

Noticeable, too, were a number of those tiny atoms of energy called little-stints – wading birds, but hardly bigger than a sparrow. They raced here and there like little mice on the sea-smoothed sand.

Farther out were other habituees of these shores – a curlew, oystercatchers and gulls, as well as several bartailed godwits, and four of what I took (in a difficult light) to be turnstones, though I associate these birds with rockier shores than Buddon sands. Curlew and turnstones are the birds in my drawing.

All these migrants were very alert and showed no sign of travel weariness. At this time some years back, however, I came upon a widespread flock of sanderlings on the wet sands at Monifieth, and they had probably encountered adverse winds. They were so tired, they scarcely moved out of my way as I walked slowly among them.

Another small flock of waders moving amidst the ripples of the incoming tide appeared to be bigger than dunlins and shorter and darker in the legs than redshanks.

Perhaps I should have known from their actions at the sea's edge that they were knots – named after the legendary King Canute, who demonstrated that even he, a king, could not halt the incoming tide.

When these birds eventually took to wing I was treated to one of those glorious displays of massed flying. At a distance the flock lightened and darkened like wind-blown draperies.

How birds can co-ordinate their movements in what (to us at least) appears to be complete silence remains a mystery, but the daring men of Leuchars could do no more!

Towards sunset a skein of wild geese came overhead, forging steadily onwards and making possibly for Loch Leven. They reminded me of marathon runners who have settled into their stride and cover mile after mile at an even pace.

Autumn sunsets at Buddon can be very beautiful – the sandbanks darkening, the sea resplendent in saffron and azure, the red sun sinking behind Broughty Castle, bronze-gold welling over half the west.

Turnstones and Curlew

December

❦

ANYONE who worked in the woods before the advent of the power-saw will know what I mean by such terms as "burnin' the hag," "sneddin'" and "barkin' the poles."

In the Longbank Woods, near Shielhill Bridge, I once asked a Kirriemuir woodsman what was meant by "sneddin'."

He lowered his axe, thoughtfully lit his pipe and got it properly going, and then said:

"It's juist ca'in the doads aff the loags."

As I was still puzzled, he then gave me a demonstration. I shall never forget it.

Wielding his axe this way and that, he moved along the trunk of a fir that had just been felled and the side branches dropped away rhythmically and magically under his expertly delivered blows.

I had a go myself, but what a hacking and whacking mess I made of it!

I decided I was better at burnin' the hag, or else sketching the trees that still raised their branches skywards.

Trees make wonderful subject-matter for sketching.

In December the bare branches and twigs are a study in themselves – some (like those of the ash) looping upwards; others (like the hawthorn and the whitebeam) clawing and scratching at the passing wind; others again (like the pendulous birch) forming a delicate tracery of twigs against the sky.

I have a great love of the Scots pine – especially those rugged veterans of the glens and moors that have withstood the storms of centuries with their gnarled trunks of roseate-grey and orange-red boughs that thrust themselves upwards into their own darkness.

Nowadays, the Scots pine is found in its truly wild state only in those fragments of the Old Caledonian Forest that remain to us here and there in the Highlands.

Yet, at one time, a vast pine forest spread over all our glens and mountains up to, and beyond, a height of 2000 feet.

Evidence is there for the seeing on our own hills and moors (Rannoch Moor, for instance) – the remains of pine trees lying in the peat-hags of what are now bare denuded uplands and treeless expanses of wind-clipped heather, moss and bog.

Many hill-walkers must have noticed these relics of a mighty race of trees – contorted roots and splintered trunks projecting from the ridges and ramparts of the rent moss, preserved in the bed of peat for thousands of years.

Possibly some great change, from a dry climate to our wet and windy one, could explain and solve one of the darkest enigmas of our Scottish hills.

Scots Pine

"ABOUT the size of a thrush, but pinky-brown and crested" was the way farmer Willie Grant, of Ardownie, described the birds that were coming to his garden and eating up the cotoneaster berries.

"I covered up the holly tree," he said, with a chuckle. "We want to keep some holly berries for Christmas."

The birds were waxwings – winter visitors from the sub-Arctic forests of Scandinavia.

Walking in deep snow along the wooded ridge from Ardownie to Ethiebeaton, I came upon several small flocks of these colourful birds – watchful but unafraid, in the wintry trees.

At close range it was easy to see the yellow tail-fringe and the waxen touch of scarlet on the wing that gives them their name.

This year's scarcity of haws may prove disastrous to the waxwing species.

It will certainly force them to come searching into gardens for any berries they can find.

Generally speaking, wild birds that find their food in the trees and hedgerows are better off in severe weather than those which feed on the ground.

Thrushes and plovers, for instance, are hard put to it when deep snow shuts their larder door.

Oddly enough, some wild birds such as blackbird, robin, tree-creeper and pheasant seem to revel in a fresh fall of snow.

But if the snow lies long it's a different story.

Then, the foxes and the crows will score, for snow renders their victims more visible, and hunger lessens their powers to escape.

Roe deer have always been fond of these wooded heights between the Panmure Monument and Ethiebeaton, although their main stronghold at the Laws (Kingennie) now stands bereft of its trees.

Roe deer are great wanderers, and woods often harbour them without the fact being known.

In one thicket, after listening to an odd sound, I found it was caused by a roe buck scraping at the snow and the mould underneath it.

The speed of the animal's forelegs as it flayed the snow was quite astonishing. At times its legs became a blur, like the spokes of a fast-moving wheel.

Up this way the snow-laden woods were like fairyland.

Mossy oak and beech stood out vividly against the snowy undergrowth, each casting a long shadow of azure on the sunlit snow.

Under their white coverlet fallen trees lay like sleeping forms.

In the lee of the hedgerows, shadows of twig and branch caught the drifts in a frail mesh of blue.

Underfoot were signs of countless birds and animals of the woods – tracks like tiny chains and bold imprints.

Here and there birds had left, not only their footmarks, but also their wing marks, and one spread-eagled impression suggested that an owl had pounced there on a mouse or vole.

If one could read all the tracks printed on the great white page of the snow, many an exciting story of the woodland folk they would tell!

Waxwings

And all the bells on earth did ring
On Christmas Day in the morning.

WE associate bells with Christmastide and joyous occasions. But the quaint little belfry that stands at Drumlithie, in the Mearns (the subject of my sketch) was built for the humbler purpose of calling the oldtime weavers to their work.

Some countries make more use of bells than we do in Scotland. Italy, for one.

In Bergamo Alta I seem to remember bells of one sort or another tinkling or clanging all day long, with a final, solemn and sonorous good-night from the dark medieval bell-tower of the old Duomo.

But still, we do have "Lang Strang" at Forfar, which can be heard across the wintry fields of Strathmore as far away as Glamis and Cortachy.

Back in the 17th century, Lang Strang (a set of three bells) was presented to Forfar by two brothers.

They were the sons of Provost Strang and they settled as merchants in Stockholm.

They never forgot their native town, however, and sent the bells as a token of their loyalty and love.

Then the bells of St John's in Perth, pealing out from the heart of the Fair City, are wonderfully joyous to hear.

And so are the bells of St Mary's in Dundee, chiming over the rooftops, and always mindful of Alice Meynell's lines :

Like birds from the cote to the gales
A flock of bells take flight.

Another bell that has always interested me stands on the ground in front of Kettins Church.

It was "pensioned off" when the church was given a new Norman tower towards the end of last century.

And there it stands, complete with its belfry, and with its metal pennant still bravely flying – its tongue ready to speak again should the need arise.

Its inscription is in Flemish.

Translated, it reads : "Maria Troon is my name. Mister Hans Popen Ruider gave me. A.D. 1519."

Not long ago I stood on Turin Hill, and looked over the frozen marshes of Restenneth to the tall spire of its priory.

It was Nechtan, King of the Picts, who brought skilled workmen from the south to raise stone churches like those of the Romans, and the first was built here at Restenneth, over 1200 years ago.

The building has been added to since then, but the square part of the tower below the broached spire is undoubtedly the oldest fragment of ecclesiastic structure in Scotland.

No doubt the priory had its own bell in bygone days, and as I stood there, with the light stooping under a shower of snow, I could easily imagine I heard it tolling softly over the midwinter landscape.

Then I thought of the ancient time,
The days of the monks of old,
When to matin and vesper and compline chime
The loud Hosanna roll'd.

Drumlithie Steeple

MEN of the fields, men of the sea, those who dwell in upland places – all are bound to know the spectacle of the northern lights or aurora borealis with more intimacy than townsfolk, whose skyline bears the limitation of wall and roof-ridge, and for whom the starry brightness must ever be dimmed by the glare of street lights.

For such auroral displays are common enough in our skies during the winter months.

Usually an eerie glow or a dim arch of light along the northern horizon is the limit of their effect, but sometimes you may see the "merry dancers" – faint rays or pencillings of light that flit and vanish and reappear.

Again there may be a curtain-like effect, with a staining of crimson or green, and many a country child has gazed in wonder and awe at this strange spectacle of the winter sky.

And there are those rare occasions when the northern lights send out great shafting streamers to comb the night sky, and set their wildly beating wings of light to fan in the far deeps of the stars.

> *The lift is fu' o' wings o' licht,*
> *Risin' and deein' doon…*

It is only on these infrequent latter occasions that townsfolk become aware of strange lights in the sky overhead.

In the same way other fine movements in nature's pageantry may pass us by – sunsets that flare and fade beyond the brick walls of our skyline, white clouds that pack and pillar into the frosty blue, rain curtains that draw and dim the trees and fields, sunlight and cloud-shadow passing across our links and moors, moonlight shining on moving, breaking seas, the silvering of the first catkins in the herald days of spring.

In the trend of modern life man has this tendency, to become separated more and more from his natural environment; so hemmed in is he by walls of his own creation, so entangled with rules and customs, tasks and laws of his own making that the open countryside and the more primary things of life might almost belong to a world apart, a dreamland of escape.

Yet "escape" is the wrong word, for this implies flight, and to turn to nature for solace and inspiration is the most natural of things.

A man does not flee back to the land of his birth, but instinctively returns to it, just as the wildfowl that cross these midwinter skies will instinctively return to their northern home when the "merry dancers" depart, and a new clear spring-light is recaptured minute by minute from the winter darkness.

The Northern Lights

Printed by Winters Pioneer Ltd, Dunsinane Industrial Estate, Dundee